D1047245

Tragic Failure

Tragic Failure

Racial Integration in America

Tom Wicker

William Morrow and Company, Inc. *New York*

It is the policy of William Morrow and Company, Inc., and its imprints and affiliates, recognizing the importance of preserving what has been written, to print the books we publish on acid-free paper, and we exert our best efforts to that end.

Library of Congress Cataloging-in-Publication Data

Wicker, Tom.
    Tragic failure : racial integration in America / Tom Wicker.—
1st ed.
        p.   cm.
    Includes bibliographical references (p.   ).
    ISBN 0-688-10629-3 (alk. paper)
    1. United States—Race relations.   2. Afro-Americans—Politics and government.   3. Afro-Americans—Economic conditions.   4. Afro-Americans—Social conditions—1975–   I. Title.
E185.615.W476   1996
305.8'00973—dc20   95-43162
                                                                          CIP

Printed in the United States of America

First Edition

1   2   3   4   5   6   7   8   9   10

BOOK DESIGN BY SUSAN HOOD

*To my grandchildren—
may they live in a better
world.*

Contents

Introduction

Sharply conflicting white and black reactions to the O. J. Simpson verdict dramatized the tragic fact that neither civil war in the nineteenth century nor the civil rights movement in the twentieth has brought racial equality, much less racial amity, to America.

I believe they can be reached only in the hearts of the people; wars will never achieve either, nor narrow legalities. Perhaps nothing can. Derrick Bell has written that African-Americans, despite surface changes in society, continue to be "the faces at the bottom of the well," the faces upon which whites, no matter how deprived themselves, can look down in the sure and comforting knowledge that at least *they* aren't black.

Having spent the first thirty-four years of my life in what was then the segregated South and the last thirty-five in what's only legally an integrated nation—and not always that—I believe the problem is not least that those black faces in the well are *reassuring* to most whites and *vital* to the self-esteem of the many disadvantaged among us, few of whom really want those faces to disappear.

The continuing separation of whites and blacks into hostile and unequal classes, however, is a fundamental cause of the political deadlock, economic inequity, and social rancor that mark American life. And if "a house divided against itself" could not stand in the era of chattel slavery, can it long endure in today's destructive atmosphere of black disadvantage, white anger, and racial animosity?

Long before O. J. Simpson went on trial, it was obvious that genuine racial equality—despite laws and legal decisions—had not been achieved in America. The high proportion of African-American* males in U.S. prisons and the low economic status of more than half the black population were evidence enough for anyone willing to see it, but few were. Even as the Simpson trial unfolded, white resentment erupted over affirmative action—an effort to overcome black disadvantages that's now widely seen, despite little evidence, as reverse racism.

When a Los Angeles jury brought in the Simpson verdict, the hard truth finally was too visible to be ignored. Whites denounced what they saw as black racial prejudice by a predominantly black jury in favor of a black hero despite the evidence. African-Americans, on the other hand, hailed black jurors for a courageous stand against white racial prejudice and constitutionally impermissible evidence provided by the racist Los Angeles police.

Throughout the long trial, "the white position [that Simpson was guilty] was treated as the rational, normal, acceptable one, David Shaw of the *Los Angeles Times* said on October 25, 1995, in a panel discussion of media coverage of the Freedom Forum. "The black perception [that Simpson was not guilty] was treated as irrational."

It's almost irrelevant the black or white judgment might be more nearly correct. In my view, what mattered was the dem-

*The author is aware that not all black Americans approve of the designation "African-American," or consider it accurate. The term is used interchangeably with "black" throughout this book, and no disrespect is intended in either case.

onstration that whites and blacks, though living in the same America, see themselves in different worlds. Similarly conflicting views were evident in the responses of African-American journalists and their mostly white supervisors to a survey question of whether U.S. press organizations are "committed to retaining and promoting black journalists." Of the white supervisors, 94 percent believed newspapers and broadcasters were so committed; 67 percent of the black (mostly middle-class) journalists thought not. Both worked in the same newsrooms; neither saw the same world of work.

The Simpson trial and verdict were followed immediately by the so-called "Million-Man March," in which at least hundreds of thousands of orderly African-American males demonstrated peacefully on the Mall in Washington in October 1995. Despite a demagogic speech by Louis Farrakhan of the Nation of Islam, the marchers espoused what white Americans, watching on television, could readily recognize as middle-class values—thus confounding the recent white view of black men as lawless and shiftless, as well as conveying the message that African-Americans still are far from equal citizenship in a supposedly integrated nation.

The march emphasized the strong growth of the black middle class in the last three decades—to perhaps 40 percent of the African-American population. Even that growth has not banished the faces from the bottom of the well, any more than it has produced real racial equality. Middle-class African-Americans testify copiously to the indignities and embarrassments they still suffer from the white assumption of black inferiority, black income and wealth still are far below white levels, housing remains largely segregated by race, and *all* African-Americans tend to be judged by the unacceptable behavior of the worst off among them.

I consider it the saddest racial development of the last quarter century that as the black middle class expanded, the urban underclass grew even faster. The scary and undisciplined behavior of that largely black underclass—those African-Americans who for lack of jobs and hope and discipline turned in the seventies and eighties to crime and welfare and drugs and were sent to prison in droves—was seen (often graphically, on television) by frightened whites as the behavior of African-Americans generally.

In one panicked and self-destructive result, whites turned against social welfare programs designed to benefit the white as well as the black poor—hence society generally. Worse, African-Americans once seen as bravely facing the police dogs and cattle prods of Bull Connor in the name of freedom came to be regarded, instead, as irresponsible muggers, drug dealers, addicts, rapists, and welfare queens.

The same period exposed the failure of the African-American political empowerment that white and black civil rights leaders of the sixties had hoped would be the remedy for black disadvantages. One of them, Dr. Kenneth Clark, sadly conceded in 1993 that greater numbers of black elected officials had been "unable to increase justice and humanity for those who have been forgotten in the inner cities."

Thirty-five years of failing integration have convinced me that economic as well as political empowerment is needed if African-American disadvantages—particularly those of the underclass—are to be overcome. Only when the faces at the bottom of the well achieve generally higher economic status might they—as well as those talented and energetic blacks in the middle class—reach genuine equality in the hearts of whites, and only through economic gains for all might the threatening underclass become a more constructive element in a more amicable American life.

Such an economic transformation will not be easily or soon accomplished, and it probably never will be if the task is left to today's major political parties. Neither any longer even talks of such ambitious goals; both are less concerned with the truly disadvantaged than with the numerically dominant white middle class, with its plaints about an unfair tax burden and unfair preferences for blacks. The Republicans offer a new home to white defectors from a Democratic party the defectors regard as too partial to blacks, and the supposedly "liberal" Democrats, alarmed by the loss of white votes, pay scant attention to the interests of African-Americans, whose allegiance causes the white defections.

In their own interest, therefore, but also in that of a racially torn nation, blacks should turn away from the Democrats to form a new party dedicated to economic equality through economic growth for whites and blacks alike. Such a new party could build upon predicted demographic change that in the next century will bring today's minority groups into rough numerical equality with non-Hispanic whites. It might even win the support of those millions of despairing Americans who now take no part in the politics of a prosperous nation they believe ruled by the affluent and for the affluent.

The new party might never win the presidency, but in the historical tradition of third parties, it could have profound effect upon the other two and upon society generally. That's why I've suggested in this book that such a radically conceived party might also have the potential to do what our old, familiar politics-as-usual never can: "To achieve real democracy—to change American life by attacking its inequities—perhaps to save us from ourselves."

Tragic Failure

1 The End of Integration

Integration is like Prohibition. If the people don't
want it, a whole army can't enforce it.

Paul Johnson,
governor of Mississippi

The sweeping conservative victory in the elections of 1994
returned control of Congress to Republicans, repudiated
what was left of liberal government, and dramatized the tragic
failure of racial integration in America.

Race, as it always is in a modern American election, was the
underlying issue. In the autumn of 1994 that issue was a prime
determinant of the outcome, as white voters everywhere expressed unmistakable yearning for a lost time, before "they"
forced themselves into the nation's consciousness.

White animosity toward and fear of African-Americans—seen
largely as criminals and welfare cheats—gave emotional edge
and added energy to the election's ostensible issues, and the campaign was fought out in code words and symbolism that disclosed rather than disguised its racial character:

- Fierce denunciations of crime and welfare, in white eyes
  the most prominent products of the black underclass
- Withering blasts at liberals and liberalism as the "social

1

engineers" behind the "big government" that tried to force racial integration and brought higher taxes
- Diatribes against "spending" and "the redistribution of wealth" to the poor, a euphemism for social programs believed primarily to aid African-Americans
- Loud promises to extend the death penalty, from which African-Americans suffer proportionally far more than whites
- Overwrought demands for a return to "family values" (a term of many meanings, one of which is the sexual restraint that blacks are supposed by whites to disdain)

Anyone who might have misunderstood what had happened in the 1994 elections should have been set straight on January 23, 1995. That day, in the ornate hearing room of the House Rules Committee, the victorious Republicans removed a portrait of former Representative Claude Pepper of Florida, a renowned white liberal Democrat. That was understandable, but the new Republican committee chairman, Gerald Solomon of New York, had ordered the Pepper portrait replaced by that of *another Democrat*, the late Howard Smith of Virginia, a last-ditch segregationist and in his many years as Rules Committee chairman one of the most powerful opponents of the civil rights legislation of the sixties.[1]

Blacks clearly believed race was the principal issue in the campaign; the reason, said Robert Smith, a professor of political science at San Francisco State University, was "absolute disgust" with the campaign among blacks of all walks.[2]

"It took us black people so long to get the vote," T. J. Smith of Philadelphia told Richard Berke of *The New York Times* in 1994. "Now they're making us not want to vote" by neglecting black interests. Chris Williams, a Philadelphia ironworker, agreed: "Why do they talk about just building jails? Why don't they talk about building schools?"[3]

The returns, if anything, left African-Americans feeling even more frustrated. Black turnout—perhaps fueled by fear—more than doubled nationally, over the 1990 midterm elections, with black voters going heavily Democratic; yet the Republicans won in a landslide and not a single Republican incumbent was defeated. Clearly, *white* voters had turned to the Republicans.

Fifty-one percent of the whites, moreover, who had responded to an election-year survey by the Times Mirror Center for the People and the Press said openly that they believed "equal rights" had been pushed too far—an increase of nine percentage points since 1992.

California, the nation's most populous state, voted by an overwhelming margin for Proposition 187, a ballot initiative designed to deprive illegal immigrants—mostly Latinos in California—of education, health, and welfare benefits. Governor Pete Wilson, whose reelection made him seem at the time a strong contender for the Republican presidential nomination, derived substantial political profit from his support for this initiative.

California's approval of Prop 187, which Democratic candidates for governor and senator opposed, may well have been symbolic of the 1994 elections as a whole. It was not an "antiblack" measure, nor was it an antiblack election *by definition*. The vote favoring Prop 187, however, clearly reflected the angry and vengeful or at least resentful racial attitudes many white Americans had developed since the high-water mark of the civil rights movement in the sixties. The entire election reflected such white attitudes.

If those attitudes reached a political peak in 1994, they had been a long time in the making. Racial integration in America had been failing for years, even though legal segregation in the southern states was ended in the sixties. The elections of 1994 only dramatized a fact that had long existed.

By that year integration had failed nationally because too few white Americans wanted it or were willing to sacrifice for it. Integration had failed too because whites' stereotypical view of blacks had been reshaped by the violence, idleness, and drug reliance of the urban black underclass. And the kind of political empowerment integration brought to blacks had proved unable to provide most African-Americans the economic and social gains needed for acceptance in white America.

The angry and fearful white reaction to undisciplined ghetto behavior also blinded whites to the concurrent growth of a substantial black middle class. Perhaps worse, that reaction had undermined white support for economic and social programs beneficial not only to the black poor but to millions of impoverished whites as well.

In actual practice, as a result of all this, integration had not been the policy of either Republican or Democratic administrations since the accession of Ronald Reagan to the presidency in 1981. In the decade before that, integration had been pursued only halfheartedly; zeal for enforcement of equal rights in education, housing, and employment had declined as antagonism to African-Americans rose.

Crime, though its victims as well as its perpetrators often were black, and welfare, widely considered a dole and an aid to shiftless blacks' supposed instinct to spawn, had long been favored targets of public and political anger.

Now the primary national approach to the ills of the urban underclass, endorsed in the polling booths of 1994, is to imprison poor blacks—an expensive, ineffective, misdirected, and self-destructive course sustained by white fear, politicians' posturing, and the sensationalism of the white press. More executions, mostly of blacks, an equally punitive and ill-considered response to crimes that already have been committed, are promised in response to the conservative landslide of 1994. Early in 1995 New York's new Republican governor, George Pataki, signed a death penalty law after nearly a quarter century of vetoes by the Democratic governors Hugh Carey and Mario Cuomo.

The inner city does teem with crime, idleness, and anger, spilling dangerously outward. Black family disintegration and welfare dependence are serious concerns. But for better or for worse, the American community necessarily *includes* the black community—African-Americans, some Latinos, many from the Caribbean. The Census Bureau predicts the black community will grow far larger. Its exclusion in anything like a democratic or humane manner would be impossible and would not solve the nation's most pressing problems; rather it would worsen some old problems and create many new ones.

Glaring economic inequities and class distinctions abound, among *both* blacks and whites. Technological or administrative competence, a prerequisite in today's economy, is seldom within the reach of poor and ill-educated Americans, of whom there are more and more of both races. Millions of whites and blacks are out of any kind of work, in the city and on the farm, and more will be in a newly competitive and technological era, with even profitable corporations laying off workers by the thousands. Manufacturing wages have declined for all. The real gap between rich and poor is widening. Unemployment, which strikes blacks first and worst, also hits whites hard—yet is fostered by a government too fearful of inflation to push economic growth strenuously and by a "lean and mean" business sector in which cost cutting has become the new panacea for all problems.

A seventh of the nation lives in poverty: more than forty million people, by no means all of them black, and including more than a fifth of all American children. Families of all races are disintegrating. The economy, measured against population growth and expected living standards, is not adequately expanding. Demographic changes predicted by the Census Bureau for the next fifty years will be of incalculable effect.

What the brash conservatives who triumphed in 1994 may be able to do about any of these troublesome truths remains, at this writing, largely to be seen. But the end of integration more or less subtly marked by their victory will not remove or diminish those ills, each of which, in large part or small, is linked to or affected by race, the continuing, the cancerous, the unconfronted American dilemma.

In the fifties and the first half of the sixties, owing mostly to effective black demonstrations and demands, the shameful institutions of legally established racial segregation in the South at last were abolished. But this shining hour for the civil rights movement proved to be brief and limited.

In the late sixties and the seventies, efforts to broaden integration into a national, not just a southern, reality caused anxiety and anger in the nonsouthern white majority. Outside the old Confederacy, integration came to be seen as moving too fast and going too far—faster and farther than most whites in the rest of the nation had expected or wanted.

A "backlash" of white resistance to civil rights quickly gathered momentum, importantly furthered by the presidential campaigns of Governor George Wallace of Alabama. The long national retreat from integration was under way within a year or two after its greatest triumphs.

Such a turnabout had hardly seemed possible in the period when antisegregation laws were being passed—slowly but, as it seemed, inevitably—by Congress under pressure from the Eisenhower, Kennedy, and Johnson administrations and over diehard southern opposition. Even, however, in the Goldwater debacle of 1964—the most smashing Democratic and liberal presidential victory since Franklin Roosevelt's in 1936—the Republicans had carried four southern states.

The old Solid South had been shattered, a development that did not surprise the victorious President Lyndon Johnson, a southerner himself. The night Congress passed the massive Civil Rights Act of 1964, proposed by President Kennedy and pushed through by Johnson, a young White House aide named Bill Moyers called the president to congratulate him on the success of the legislation.

"Bill," Johnson replied, "I think we Democrats just lost the South for the rest of my life."

Inasmuch as LBJ died in 1972, it turned out to be for considerably longer than that. In 1994, thirty years later, the Democratic share of the vote in House races in the South dropped to 13.4 percent of eligible voters.

To most observers in 1964—including Tom Wicker, a *New York Times* political reporter—the southern defections had seemed relatively unimportant. After all, LBJ had defeated

Goldwater by 486 to 52 in the electoral college. The Republicans had carried only one state (Goldwater's Arizona) outside the South, had lost 38 seats in the House and retained only 140, their lowest total since 1936. They also had lost 2 Senate seats and held only 32, no more than they had had in 1940. Republican defeats in state and local elections had been so severe as to cause frequent laments that the GOP was no longer an effective national party.

Only two years later, in a vigorous 1966 campaign led by Richard M. Nixon (out of office since 1961 but obviously on the road back), Republicans picked up forty-seven House seats, three in the Senate, and eight governorships, most significantly in California, where the political newcomer and old movie star Ronald Reagan first won political office. The Republican comeback was marked by a superb organizing and fund-raising effort in the wake of Goldwater's defeat and by Nixon's leadership. But it benefited above all from *the Democratic party's and Johnson's racial liberalism.*

The president and his party had pushed through the Civil Rights Act of 1964, guaranteeing equal access to public facilities and banning racial discrimination in the workplace. They had achieved the Voting Rights Act of 1965, putting the federal government behind blacks' right to vote. Johnson himself had proclaimed to Congress the battle cry of Martin Luther King and his followers: "We shall overcome!" LBJ and John F. Kennedy rather reluctantly before him had identified their party more closely with African-Americans than any president since Lincoln.

Three decades later, in his 1995 inaugural speech as the new Republican Speaker of the House, Newt Gingrich—magnanimously praising the opposition, or so it appeared—noted that Democrats had been "the greatest leaders in fighting for an integrated America." He added pointedly: "It was the liberal wing of the Democratic party that ended segregation."

These honeyed words, intentionally or not, were political poison. Voters had shown in 1994 and earlier that they were well aware, and not favorably, of the Democrats' racial record. It had been apparent for years that this record was a political liability not just in the South but with the nation's white majority.

In early 1964, the year of Goldwater's defeat, a Gallup poll had found that 72 percent of nonsouthern whites believed the Johnson administration's pace toward civil rights was "about right" or even too slow. But as civil rights legislation began to touch life *outside* the South, although it had been expected generally that only the old Confederacy would be much affected, nonsouthern whites began to fear for property values, job security, local government, neighborhood cohesion—for the old, inherited, comfortable (for them) order of things.

By 1966 opinion surveys were showing a startling reversal: Three quarters of white voters thought blacks were moving ahead too fast, demanding and "being given" too much, at the expense of whites. As white backlash mounted, polls the next year suggested that "the number one concern" of most respondents was fear that black gains would damage the well-being of whites. And as the decade continued, blacks rioting in the cities—fearfully or angrily watched by a nation becoming addicted to television—and blacks raising clenched fists in the black power salute seemed not only threatening but ungrateful for white "concessions" (as whites tended to see changes in the old racial order).

The black separatist and "black is beautiful" movements, the anti-integrationist rhetoric of Malcolm X, the militant stance and demands of organizations like the Black Panthers and the Student Nonviolent Coordinating Committee (SNCC) all stirred white animosity and anxiety. So did aggressive African-Americans like H. Rap Brown, Stokely Carmichael, Huey Newton, and Bobby Seale. The student and anti-Vietnam demonstrations were assumed by many whites to be a predictable consequence of black protests. Crime was increasing, much of it perpetrated by poor blacks, with television dramatizing it in the living room.

In 1967, as a result of the urban riots, President Johnson appointed a bipartisan commission, chaired by Governor Otto Kerner of Illinois, to look into the riots' causes. After extensive inquiry the Kerner Commission dismissed the notion that integration was proceeding too swiftly. Its report contended instead that despite the apparent success of the civil rights movement, black disadvantages still were so overwhelming that "our nation is moving toward two societies, one black, one white—separate but unequal."

Many prominent Americans, white and black, shared and approved this view, but many others resented it. Hadn't enough already been done for blacks? Even Lyndon Johnson, with a presidential election impending and the nation alarmed at what many believed to be insurrection in the cities, disliked the commission's conclusion and might have disavowed it if he could have. The backlash was not reversed; the riots undoubtedly heightened it.

Thus in 1968 fear and resentment of African-Americans underlay the "law and order" issue loudly demagogued by George Wallace and more subtly exploited by Richard Nixon in the "southern strategy" by which he narrowly won the presidency. The national loss of confidence in "Johnson's war" in Vietnam and destructive divisions within the party hurt the Democrats. But primarily, I believe, it was white racial anxieties that brought disaster to the party of Kennedy and Johnson only four years after its greatest victory. And the black community's impressive gains were becoming the cause of alarming losses of white support for the Democrats.

Wallace campaigned widely and effectively, using code words and flamboyant oratory to stimulate white fears and to castigate the federal government. He finished a relatively distant third in the 1968 election, receiving votes from Democrats deserting the old civil rights advocate Hubert Humphrey and from Republicans who preferred Wallace's tough talk to Nixon's subtler appeal to white sentiment. In retrospect, however, Wallace's campaign was one of the most consequential of the postwar years. It effectively moved the country to the right, making racial fears seem more legitimate and paving the way for Ronald Reagan to win the presidency twelve years later.

Nixon's election and Wallace's campaign in 1968 sped along the national retreat from integration (though the courts forced President Nixon to push southern school desegregation in 1970).

During the seventies affirmative action and "busing" were widely resented, even in Boston, once the seat of abolitionism. Low-income whites who could not afford private schools for their children and who felt their job security threatened by new competition from minority groups and women were especially alienated.

The Democrats and the integration they had pushed and supported were blamed for these perceived threats to the established order. Twenty-four years of Republican and conservative ascendancy, broken only briefly and feebly by Jimmy Carter's single presidential term (1977–81),* followed the election of 1968 with near inevitability.

During the seventies escalating fears of busing, affirmative action, and neighborhood breakdown caused many whites to see integration not as laudable national policy but as "racism in reverse." The deterioration of cities and the increase in crime and violence were largely blamed on blacks. This development of the newly visible underclass, moreover, sharpened white fear and anger.

Whites continued to look down at the black "faces at the bottom of society's well,"[4] those "magical faces" of which Derrick Bell has written that "[e]ven the poorest whites, those who must live their lives only a few levels above, gain their self-esteem by gazing down at us." Those black faces had always been there, viewed merely with contempt and complacency by some, with bitter relief by the poor, the disadvantaged, the despised, who had little of value but their white skins. Despite civil rights laws, surely those "faces at the bottom of the well" always would be there.

Their absence would announce to whites not just the end of segregation in the South but the arrival of an all but unimaginable new world, making life less comfortable for some whites,

*Carter's narrow victory over Gerald Ford derived mostly from reaction against the Watergate scandal of the Nixon years and Ford's pardon of Nixon himself. Without those counterbalancing factors, the Democrats might well have lost the close election of 1976 too, owing to the party's racial record and Carter's relatively liberal stance.

nearly unbearable for others. And those black faces imposed a double imperative on whites: Not only must they be kept at the bottom of the well, but those who would bring them to the top, or nearer to it, must be feared, castigated, opposed.

And then came Reagan.

On August 3, 1980, looking virile and businesslike, he spoke in shirtsleeves to a cheering crowd of about ten thousand people, nearly all white, at the Neshoba County Fairgrounds near Philadelphia, Mississippi.

"I believe in states' rights," Reagan declared that day in the well-modulated voice that was to become so familiar to Americans. The Republican presidential nominee then promised a restoration to the states and to local governments of "the power that properly belongs to them."

Fresh from his Republican National Convention victory at Detroit, Ronald Reagan was making the first formal appearance of his presidential campaign, and his choice of a site for that opening appearance was powerfully symbolic: Philadelphia, Mississippi, was the place where three volunteer civil rights workers in the Mississippi Summer Project of 1964, two Jews and a black—Andrew Goodman, Michael Schwerner, and James Chaney—had been murdered. The sheriff and deputy sheriff of Neshoba County had been charged with these crimes. Most of the county's white population, by its silence, had been either complicit or oblivious.

No presidential candidate before Reagan had visited remote Neshoba County, in a state that had been the last stronghold of resistance to blacks' civil rights. Reagan was there because a Mississippi member of Congress, Trent Lott (now the assistant Republican leader in the Senate), had assured him that a personal visit to the state would carry it for him against President Carter.

The candidate might not fully have grasped the significance of Philadelphia, as later he would not understand the opposition to his visit to the Bitburg Cemetery in Germany, where members of the Nazi SS were buried. But if Reagan didn't know about

Philadelphia, Mississippi, he should have. It could not conceivably have been a routine campaign stop. One week after the bodies of Goodman, Schwerner, and Chaney had been discovered buried in a nearby earthen dam in 1964, Governor Paul Johnson—without a word of sympathy for the dead youths or their families—had told a crowd of six thousand at the Neshoba County fair that no Mississippian, including state officials, had any obligation to obey the Civil Rights Act of 1964.

"Integration," Johnson declaimed, "is like Prohibition. If the people don't want it, a whole army can't enforce it."[5]

In 1964 that was the voice of last-ditch resistance, soon to be overwhelmed by events. But by 1980, as Ronald Reagan stood where the governor had stood, looking out upon much the same sea of white faces, it was possible to see Paul Johnson as a national prophet, no longer as a southern relic. Reagan's mere appearance at Philadelphia—unthinkable for a major-party presidential candidate even a few years earlier—was evidence that times had changed, radically. And when the candidate chose to open his campaign where Schwerner, Chaney, and Goodman had made the last sacrifice to rabid segregationist resistance, he sent the nation a message many Americans *wanted* to hear. That message was far more powerful and far more convincing than the deceptive plausibility with which Reagan was later to call for a "color-blind society" and insist that he was "heart and soul in favor of the things that have been done in the name of civil rights and desegregation. . . ."

Reagan's actual policies exposed those words as lip service, and anyway, much of the nation was watching what he did—visiting Philadelphia, Mississippi, for instance—rather than listening to what he said. Even before his speech at Philadelphia, Reagan had openly opposed the Civil Rights Act of 1964, the Voting Rights Act of 1965, the Open Housing Act of 1968 and in numerous other ways had demonstrated his fundamental opposition to the *fact*, if not the concept, of integration. And by the time he sought the presidency—nearly winning the Republican nomination in 1976, taking it easily in 1980—neither his clear anti-integration record nor even his appearance in Mississippi was a political liability. It was, in fact, largely *because* of these that Ronald Reagan was elected to the White House.

Reagan did not single-handedly and from his own convictions turn the nation against integration. Rather a national reversal had begun not long after the civil rights triumphs of the sixties and his own entry into public life in California. In those years, as outlined above, national reluctance—neither confined to the South nor always most pronounced there—moved steadily toward opposition to integration. That movement owed more to crime, the underclass, busing, affirmative action, and *fear* (as much of the unknown as of any observable phenomena) than to the words or deeds of any one politician, even George Wallace. Reagan benefited politically from a greatly changed public mood even as he contributed to that mood.

Once he was in the Oval Office, moreover, the anti–civil rights record Reagan accumulated was so lengthy and substantial that he could not have compiled it without the acquiescence and support of white Americans. "From Philadelphia to the Bitburg cemetery to the veto on sanctions against South Africa," Jesse Jackson observed toward the end of the Reagan years, "it's one unbroken ideological line."[6]

That was true enough, but it was also true that Reagan had read accurately a public mood of disenchantment with racial integration. If even a beloved president thought blacks were being "given too much," as his actions (if not always his words) suggested, then surely ordinary Americans could think so too.

With tacit support from a popular president, it became respectable for whites to express loudly their misgivings about integration and to act on their fearful or hostile instincts about black neighbors or employees or schoolmates or job competitors. Those misgivings were many and fierce, those instincts had been frequently offended; so all too many white Americans were grateful that Reagan seemed to share their views. They took full advantage of what seemed to be approval from the top.

2 No Chair in the White House

We have to simply, calmly, methodically reassert
American civilization.

Newt Gingrich

Sometime in the eighties Vernon Jordan, the prominent
black attorney, later a close adviser to President Clinton,
was turned away from a bar in Florida, though the white
men he was with were admitted. A white woman barring the
door and her husband were adamant, and when Jordan cited
the public accommodations law in force since 1964, the woman
told him she "didn't care." Sounding like an echo from the old
days of segregation, she added: "You let one in, you have to let
'em all in."

Jordan concluded that she had been "encouraged indirectly"
to act as she did "because of what she heard coming out of
Washington" from the Reagan administration.[1]

President Reagan virtually had to be forced to support effective
renewal and strengthening of even the Voting Rights Act, a
measure hard to consider a threat to a "color-blind society." It
does, of course, promote equality through enforced voting rights

for African-Americans and thus is considered by some—incredibly to others—to be a "racial preference."

Reagan claimed with his accustomed brand of sincerity that he was "in complete sympathy with the goals and purposes" of the voting rights legislation. What patriotic American could not be? He nevertheless professed to see in it "flaws and faults" that he said were dangerous enough to cause him to oppose renewal altogether. He even suggested that the bill "humiliated the South,"[2] without reference to the humiliations for so long suffered by southern blacks turned away from the voting booth.

As promised in the 1980 Republican platform, on which he had been elected, Reagan reversed the policy of the Internal Revenue Service that had denied federal tax exemption to private schools practicing racial discrimination. Ostensibly he acted on the grounds that the IRS had usurped powers beyond those authorized by Congress; in fact, he sought to show his doubts about school integration by protecting new forms of segregated education (and, not so incidentally, to repay southern political supporters).

Before Reagan could manage to appoint a majority of the Supreme Court, however, that court overruled him in the Bob Jones University case and brought to an end his dogged effort to help finance the many segregated "May 17 academies" in the South.*

The Reagan administration held out as long as possible against authorizing a federal holiday on Martin Luther King's birthday, a proposal to which many white voters also objected, and still do. Recognizing rising public fear of affirmative action, the president opposed "goals and timetables," insisting that these were the same as "quotas." He and Clarence Thomas, the black conservative he appointed director of the Equal Employment Opportunity Commission, effectively neutered the agency by disallowing class action suits, forcing each discrimination charge

---

*So called by H. L. Gates, the director of Harvard's black studies program. It was on May 17, 1954, that Chief Justice Earl Warren read the Supreme Court decision that ruled segregated public schools unconstitutional.

to be independently investigated and proved. This time-consuming policy burdened the EEOC with an unmanageable backlog that existed long after Reagan had left office and his successor had promoted Thomas to the federal bench.

Reagan and his assistant attorney general for civil rights, the flinty William Bradford Reynolds,* even attempted to roll back court-imposed school desegregation plans, actually succeeding in Norfolk, Virginia. Reagan refused to impose economic sanctions on South Africa for its apartheid policy and was visibly reluctant to support his own administration's agencies when they tried to enforce civil rights policies, as they were legally bound to do.

No president could have compiled such a record in the face of vigorous public *support* for further measures of racial integration or even for those already existing in 1981. Newspaper editorial pages, minority groups, liberal Democrats in and out of office, a few dogged "Eisenhower Republicans," and plenty of voters, white as well as black, *did* oppose Reagan's policies, sometimes successfully, as when he tried to grant tax exemption to segregated private schools. But his sometimes subtle, sometimes open anti-integration approach was sufficiently in accord with the public mood that he apparently profited politically, as demonstrated by his landslide reelection in 1984 and his continuing popularity.

Important as Reagan's actions—or lack of them—were, the president's and his administration's *attitudes,* foretold at Philadelphia, Mississippi, in 1980, spoke with equal force. Reagan himself refused to meet with the Black Caucus of members of the House of Representatives, despite its repeated requests for an audience. When the Black Leadership Forum asked to meet with the president, Ed Meese—later Reagan's attorney general but then the White House deputy chief of staff—invited the

---

*Reynolds, who failed to win Senate confirmation when Reagan tried to make him deputy attorney general, once was described by Benjamin Hooks, then the executive director of the NAACP, as a "latter-day Bilbo." Theodore Bilbo had been an unabashed racist senator from Mississippi.

forum's sixteen members as individuals, not as a formal body, to Blair House across Pennsylvania Avenue from the White House, a none-too-subtle form of segregation. The president himself did not attend, and nothing of substance was accomplished.

Again, when a meeting on drug abuse policy was held in the Reagan White House, no invitation was extended to Representative Charles Rangel of New York, a recognized congressional specialist on the subject but an African-American. A spokesman lamely explained that "no chair" was available for Rangel at the White House!

Reagan had to take much liberal and journalistic derision in these instances. But he was not, in fact, defying public opinion. He was reading it more accurately than his political opposition and most commentators did and exploiting it more skillfully than they realized.

Worse than his specifically racial actions and attitudes, worse for most whites as well as for African-Americans, were Reagan's economic policies, by which the rich got richer and the poor got poorer. This trend struck not solely but hardest at black families, psychologically as well as actually.

In 1969, when the Democrats had yielded the White House to Nixon, twenty-four million Americans, many of them black, were living in poverty. That was bad enough, but then antipoverty progress began to slow. By 1986, midway through Reagan's second term, Americans living in poverty, including an outsize proportion of African-Americans, numbered more than thirty-two million.[3]

By 1987, moreover, the nation's wealth and income had been more narrowly concentrated: one half of 1 percent of Americans held 26.9 percent of the wealth. Not many of them were black. The top 10 percent of households controlled about 60 percent of the wealth, but not many of them were black either. Reagan's "supply-side" tax rate cuts of 1981, combined with the Democrats' capital gains tax reduction of 1978, was one good reason; together they reduced the "effective overall, combined federal tax rate paid by the top 1 percent of Americans" (who numbered few, if any, blacks) from 30.9 percent in 1977 to 23.1 percent in 1984.[4]

In contrast, the percentage of total money income received by the poorest fifth of the population dropped through the Reagan years: from 5.1 in 1980 to 4.6 in 1988. That fifth did include lots of African-Americans. In the same years the percentage of money income received by the wealthiest fifth of the population rose from 41.6 to 44 percent.

By 1987 median family income, which had plummeted in the early eighties, had barely recovered to the level of 1973, fourteen years earlier: about $31,000. The after-tax median in 1987 was well below the levels of the late seventies. In the years 1977–88 the average family income of the poorest tenth of Americans, obviously including many blacks, fell from $4,113 to $3,504, and only the wealthiest two tenths of Americans enjoyed an increase in average family income. But the richest 1 percent's average family income rose by *49.8 percent*, to $404,566.

Children were hard hit by declining income levels. By 1995, American children were poorer than those of any other Westernized industrial nation. The income gap in the United States between the richest and poorest children was about $55,000 a year. Families of four that were poorer than 90 percent of other such families were earning only $10,923 annually.[5]

Long after Reagan had departed from the White House, another economic study[6] concluded that the United States had less "economic equality" than any industrialized society, including class-stratified Britain. The study cited Federal Reserve figures from 1989 (when Reagan left office) to show that the richest 1 percent of American households in that year held 39 percent of the nation's wealth, leaving only 61 percent of national wealth for all the other 99 percent of the people, which included virtually all African-Americans. Annual income levels in the United States also were shown as badly skewed: The top 20 percent of income-earning households had taken in 55 percent of all after-tax income in 1989, while the lowest 20 percent, in which most blacks were to be found, received only 5.7 percent of after-tax income.

The study ignored whatever benefits Medicaid and food

stamps bring to the poor, as well as some other government programs and employer pension plans. It also obscured the fact that many young people earn more as they grow older and that Americans' incomes can change sharply from one year to the next. But these fluctuations usually occur within the middle or affluent classes and seldom represent a rags-to-riches change. And even if income and wealth disparities are present and increasing in most generous welfare states, they are extreme in the United States and underline economic and political policies—not least Reagan's—that favor the well-off over the poor and thus have a disproportionate racial effect.

These divisive approaches are not lost on many disadvantaged Americans, including blacks, and the consequences can be damaging to the nation. As Robert Greenstein of the Center on Budget and Policy Priorities has observed, "When you have a child poverty rate that is four times the average of Western European countries that are our principal industrial competitors, and when those children are a significant part of our future work force, you have to worry about the competitive effects as well as the social-fabric effects."[7]

While some of the causes of economic disparities may lie outside government policies—falling manufacturing wages owing to automation, for example—others result directly from political decisions. Examples are the relatively low minimum wage and the favorable tax rates for the rich that Reagan pushed in the 1980s. And neither Democratic nor Republican leaders today are devoting themselves to programs that might narrow income and wealth gaps.

Here is an example of the racial effect of economic policy: The black middle class (defined as persons having incomes two to five times the poverty level) grew from 20 percent of the total African-American population in 1960 to 38 percent in the early seventies, nearly doubling in little more than a decade. But more than another decade later, in 1987–88, near the end of the Reagan years, the growth of the black middle class had reached to only 43 percent of the total black population, a mere five percentage points above the early seventies level.[8]

And even though affirmative action had been given its strongest push by a Republican, President Richard Nixon, in the so-called Philadelphia Plan,* Reagan made clear his opposition to that too. Employers everywhere understood that hiring pressure from Washington had slackened. College administrations certainly got the message: From 4.3 percent of full-time faculty at American institutions of higher education in 1979, the black proportion *dropped* to 4.1 percent in 1985. It had recovered only to 4.5 percent by 1989, as the Reagan administration came to an end, so that in ten years of supposed integration only a minuscule percentage gain in numbers of black faculty in higher education had been achieved. That was forty-five years after the Supreme Court's decision desegregating public schools.[9]

The Reagan administration also killed another Nixon program: revenue sharing, a redistribution of federal funds to the states and cities. Urban blacks had benefited substantially from revenue sharing—for instance, in recreational and health care facilities. But Ronald Reagan had opposed revenue sharing all the way back to his years as governor of California, and when he got his chance in Washington, he killed it.

The 1987 report of the Urban League summed up the effect on blacks of just six years of Reagan economic policies: "Black family income has declined, poverty rates have increased, and the labor market difficulties of blacks have intensified. Moreover, social inequality in income, employment and wages has also increased. On the national level, six years of Reagan policies have produced no gains for blacks."[10]

That was written nearly a quarter century after *Brown* v. *Board of Education of Topeka, Kansas* had started the process of integration in America.

"It's almost," Eddie N. Williams, the African-American director of the Joint Center for Political Studies, said at about that time, "as if the words 'black America' are not part of [Reagan's] lexicon."[11] He might have added that those words had all but

---

*A reference to the city in Pennsylvania, not the hamlet in Mississippi.

fallen out of the nation's vocabulary as well—except when the blame was being passed around for crime and welfare.

George Herbert Walker Bush of Andover and Yale lacked Ronald Reagan's easy, empty charm, for which Bush's white-shoe "preppiness" was a poor substitute. But like Reagan, Bush had opposed the Civil Rights Act of 1964, the major instrument in the abolition of legal segregation. Like Barry Goldwater, he had voted as a member of Congress (from Texas) in 1964 to *defeat* the act. And when Bush succeeded Reagan in the White House in 1989, his presidential campaign, in a TV ad that shamelessly exploited white racial fears of marauding blacks, had inscribed the name of Willie Horton on the national nervous system.

Though he once had billed himself as a moderate, Bush feared and perhaps exaggerated the power of the right wing that dominated Republican party conventions and loved Ronald Reagan. Bush had opposed Reagan in 1980 but then had become his willing subordinate as vice president. The Republican right probably never would have accepted the eastern patrician Bush had he appeared to be anything but a loyal Reagan disciple.

His political mutation therefore served ample notice that his policies and attitudes toward African-Americans would not be much different from those of 1981-89. They weren't, nor was the public mood of indifference, verging into hostility, toward blacks' problems and aspirations.

In the same White House from which Lyndon Johnson had led the fight for the Civil Rights Act of 1964 and the Voting Rights Act of 1965, Bush fought to the bitter end a losing battle against what became the Civil Rights Act of 1991. It had been written primarily to reverse what the Democratic Congress considered faulty Supreme Court interpretations of congressional intent in previous civil rights measures.

Bush, however, falsely invoked one of the knee-jerk words of white reaction. He called the legislation a quota bill—against the considered judgment of virtually every qualified authority on civil rights or economic measures, including such outstanding members of his own party as the former Ford administration Cabinet officer William Coleman, an African-American. In this instance Bush's repeated use of the word "quota" probably heightened what no doubt would have been in any case the public's substantial antipathy to the bill.

Worse, politically, was Bush's seeming indifference to the recession of the early nineties, the primary cause of his precipitate decline in popularity from the heights he had reached during the Gulf War. Inaction against recession hurt more whites than blacks and probably was the major cause of Bush's defeat by Bill Clinton in November 1992. But that defeat came too late for black workers and families that had suffered disproportionately—as they already had in the Reagan years—from the economic decline that Bush did little to reverse or ease.

Bush did not even propose the kind of countercyclical economic measures that had been taken to fight recessions during the Ford (Republican) and Carter (Democratic) administrations. He made no effort to provide emergency public service jobs or public works, nor did he offer or seem to recognize the need for programs to offset economic dislocations in urban areas. The political scientist Demetrios Caraley has pointed out that if the antirecession legislation voted by Congress in 1976 (when Gerald Ford was president) and 1977 (with Jimmy Carter in the White House) had been reenacted in the early 1990s, seventeen billion 1990 dollars would have been made available to sustain the economy.

Bush also continued Reagan's policy of cutting back federal government support for urban programs, reductions that hit hardest at African-Americans, who are twice as likely as whites to live in central cities, particularly those cities with serious economic problems.[12] Direct aid to cities for urban mass transit, for public service jobs and training, for compensatory education, for social services and economic development—all of substantial value to urban blacks—was reduced in the Reagan and Bush years, to the point where the federal share of city budgets fell from 18 percent in 1980 to 6.4 percent in 1990.

John Lindsay, a former mayor of New York, a former Republican, and a member of the Kerner Commission that investigated the urban riots of the late sixties, estimated in 1993 that the Reagan and Bush administrations had denied New York City alone about twenty billion dollars in federal aid that it might previously have received.* Coupled with declining city revenues resulting from economic recession and the outmigration of urban populations, the reduced federal aid predictably caused sharp cutbacks in urban services and sharp increases in urban deficits—and occasionally in urban taxes. None of that was helpful to the black community.

Bush's economic policies aroused widespread opposition, however, not so much because they were devastating to African-Americans as because they severely damaged white Americans, far more visibly than had Reagan's favor-the-rich approach. A man being laid off from his job, a woman unable to afford food for her family, are likely to be angrier about this than someone reading about the decline of taxes on the wealthy, especially since one of the persistent characteristics of Americans is that so many expect, or at least hope, someday to be rich themselves. Blacks are not immune to this often foolish optimism.

Bush strained credulity when he nominated the conservative Clarence Thomas to replace the revered African-American leader Thurgood Marshall on the Supreme Court, terming Thomas "the best-qualified man" for the post, when it was well known that Thomas had little experience in the law. The nominee nevertheless received substantial African-American support, apparently owing to racial solidarity rather than to any visible concern on his part about his sponsor's economic and other policies.

After the Los Angeles riots of 1992, Bush cruised loftily past damaged areas in a limousine, seldom alighting to talk with Angelenos, mostly black and Hispanic in those neighborhoods. In one television interview he even seemed to deny that the riots

---

*Lindsay spoke at a conference in Albany, New York, honoring the Kerner Report twenty-five years after it had been issued.

had been in any way a protest against social or economic conditions. What the nation had seen on TV, he said, was "the brutality of a mob, pure and simple." Many whites no doubt agreed or were persuaded by the president's words that the riots amounted to no more than that.

For blacks, the Urban League's 1991 report aptly described the economic situation that Bush had done so little to reverse:

> Both in absolute terms and in comparison to white Americans, blacks have high unemployment rates, low rates of employment, inferior occupational distributions, and low wages and earnings. Blacks have low incomes and high poverty rates. They own little wealth and small amounts of business property.... [T]he disparities in all the above-mentioned measures of economic status have persisted at roughly the same level for the last two decades, and many indicators of inequality have even drifted upwards.... [13]

The plight of black America, however, was not the cause of George Bush's defeat in November 1992 by Bill Clinton and the Democrats. That issue, if it *was* an issue, was hardly raised by the victors. Bush failed to win reelection to the White House primarily because he had lost sight of whites' interests too.

William Jefferson Clinton showed himself in the first half of his term to be a weak president, unable to push through important legislation and retreating before strong opposition. His efforts, moreover, were more nearly focused, as had been suggested by his "new Democrat" campaign of 1992, on *middle-class* rather than underclass or black concerns or those of poor whites.

Clinton's crime bill called for more prisons, more police, more death penalties, and when in Memphis in 1993 he addressed one of the most divisive of racial issues, black crime, he offered no practical assistance to the black community but urged African-

Americans in passionate moral terms to be better than they are—
better, for that matter, than many whites are.*

After the 1994 elections, in which the Republican triumph
nearly repudiated Clinton's leadership, he almost immediately
called for a tax cut to benefit the middle class, not for new
approaches to aid the disadvantaged. He obviously had been
reading the election returns.

Fifty-two percent of those voting in the 1994 House elections
had opted for the Republican Contract with America, thus dem-
onstrating dissatisfaction with Clinton and the Democrats and
returning Republican majorities to control of both houses of
Congress. The conservative contract, however, had not appealed
to voters because it offered much hope for the less affluent of
either race. Quite the opposite. The contract pledged tax reduction for the middle class, a balanced federal budget, and severe
cuts in social programs, particularly welfare. It clearly was an
appeal to white, middle-class Americans and proved hugely successful. To these, and even to true-blue conservatives, however,
its success at the polls may prove as illusory as Clinton's 1992
victory was for liberals.

The contract's clichés and simplicities addressed a number of
difficult problems—reducing crime, welfare dependency, and
teenage births, for instance. These would not yield easily to *any*
remedy. And by mid-1995 the Senate had rejected a House-
bpassed constitutional amendment to require a balanced federal
budget. The new Republican House majority had reneged on its
pledge to impose term limits on politicians, become bogged
down in conflicting proposals for providing a line-item veto for
the president, and was engaged in a potentially suicidal inter-
necine fight over whether to emphasize "moral issues" supported
by the powerful and aggressive "religious right"—such issues as
opposition to abortion and support for prayer in the schools—
or more traditional and less divisive economic measures of conservatism.

*See Chapter Ten for a fuller discussion of the Memphis speech and its
implications.

By then, too, Democrats, including Clinton, seemed to be scoring politically with their charge that the Republican majorities planned to cut such programs as Medicare for the old and the sick (white as well as black) so that they could further reduce taxes on the rich (mostly white). Many Americans appeared to be alarmed by the Republicans' vehemently expressed faith in "the market" and in private benevolence to replace government regulation and programs; these attitudes seemed to threaten—or promise, depending on one's view—a return to a pre-1933, pre–New Deal economy and society, *before* Social Security, market and banking regulations, welfare, environmental regulation, and numerous other federal social programs long established by 1995.

Whether Americans ultimately would reward the party that destroyed or limited these long-standing monuments benefiting so many of them was by no means clear.

In July 1995, an informal survey found voters uneasy in Tennessee—a state Clinton carried in 1992 but which elected two Republican senators and a Republican governor in 1994. These voters were not convinced either that Republican ascendancy would last or that Republican legislation would bring about the fundamental change they had voted for in November 1994.

Rawls Ray, a fifty-year-old computer operator, observed that "a lot of distrust among the voters" still existed, and added: "If you have the right Democrat out there next time, I'll vote for him."[14]

In November 1995, a year after the great victory for the Contract with America, scattered state and local election returns showed few further Republican gains. No definite trend could be discerned but Democrats did elect a governor in Kentucky and retain control of the Virginia legislature, despite a major Republican effort to take it over.

The lesson of George Bush in 1992 was perhaps instructive: What happened to Medicare and food stamps and school lunches and the environment would affect more whites than African-Americans.

The new Republican approach was obvious and soon demonstrated: Big, liberal, redistributionist, bureaucratic government and its welfare programs would be cut down or abolished. The deficit would be eliminated, and a tax cut paid for, by cutting or abolishing liberal programs established and maintained by the New Deal and its successors.

The contract never promised to provide employment, boost wages, invest in the schools or job training, offer drug rehabilitation, control handguns, or improve health care—all items of interest to the inner city and to the poor generally. Workable alternatives to welfare were not detailed, only pledged. Programs intended to *prevent* crime were sneered at and earmarked for extinction. The contract instead offered more severe punishment for criminals, as if the United States were not already second in the world in the number of people it imprisons and the rate at which it incarcerates them.

Newt Gingrich, the white congressman from Georgia and the originator of the contract, whose reelection resulted in his becoming Speaker of the House and de facto Republican party leader, personally emphasized the contract's clear intent in a confident victory speech. African-Americans could take little comfort from his words.

"It is impossible," he told a Washington audience on November 11, 1994,[15] "to take the Great Society structure of bureaucracy, the redistributionist model of how wealth is acquired and the counterculture values that now permeate how we deal with the poor, and have any hope of fixing things. They are a disaster. They have ruined the poor. They create a culture of poverty and a culture of violence. And they have to be replaced thoroughly."

In one sentence Gingrich had rung bells all the way back to the now-derided sixties in denouncing the "counterculture," to Lyndon B. Johnson and the flowering of the civil rights movement in referring contemptuously to the Great Society, and even to New Deal social concerns in disdaining "the redistributionist model of how wealth is acquired." Suburban, middle-class, white America, clearly the prime victor in the 1994 elections, tends to associate all of the above with African-Americans.

In another sentence the Speaker-to-be linked "the poor"—frequently nowadays a reference to the black underclass—with "cultures" of poverty and violence, promising bluntly to "replace" them. And "we have to say to the counterculture," he proclaimed, as if it still existed, " 'Nice try. You failed. You're wrong.' And we have to simply, calmly, methodically reassert American civilization."

We have to go back, he might as well have said, to a more orderly time before the "counterculture"—before the liberals and the civil rights movement brought desegregation, welfare, crime, and violence to the nation.

Then, in a coda repeating his oft-stated 1994 campaign theme, Gingrich declared it "impossible to maintain civilization with 12-year-olds having babies, 15-year-olds killing each other, 17-year-olds dying of AIDS and with 18-year-olds ending up with diplomas they can barely read."

These were not references to the children of white Republicans in Gingrich's Georgia congressional district; every one of the cited trends is primarily associated in white minds with the black ghetto—though not usually with African-Americans' long history of repression, discrimination, and disdain or with the more recent white political abandonment of the underclass.

Thus Gingrich and the Contract with America seemed to say: "Liberalism created the ghetto with its crime and violence and welfare, so eliminating liberalism will eliminate those creations too." Racial integration, they did not need to add, was another of liberalism's products. Killing them all would begin to restore American civilization to the good old days.

Clearly, and despite Clinton's election to the presidency in 1992 (a political aberration, as was that of Jimmy Carter in 1976), the 1994 midterm elections restored and furthered the prevailing political trend of the last two decades: toward the end of integration. That trend is unlikely to be reversed anytime soon—at least not until the people want it to be.

At the same time polls show both parties and most institutions of government to be held by the public in varying degrees of disrespect. Both parties are reliant on, indebted to, and protective of powerful corporate interests. Their individual members are too fearful of defeat at the polls to support radical economic change of benefit to the poor of both races. The reigning Republicans are devoted primarily to serving the immediate wishes of the mostly white middle class. The Democrats, from Bill Clinton down, have become the "me too" party, with neither the power nor the vision, nor perhaps the political courage, to advance the interests of poor African-Americans and poor whites.

Yet if the nation is to achieve the racial reconciliation vital to a secure future, economic change should be the first and most important step. That's why the stage seems now to be set for the emergence of a new political party, one principally dedicated to the inclusion of all Americans of all races in a generous economy and a just society.

3 Mainstream to Nowhere

There ain't a dime's worth of difference between
the Democrats and the Republicans.

George C. Wallace

If racial integration is to be revived as essential to a secure
future for America, an effective new political party forthrightly working for economic justice will be necessary. The most
important step toward that goal would be the weaning of
African-Americans from their overwhelming modern allegiance
to the Democratic party. It won't be easy, but it might be done.

A new American political party dedicated to expanded economic opportunity and greater social inclusion might well be
based on:

- The growing populations of what are now called minority
  groups, which will be much larger in the future
- The existing nucleus of liberals and nonconservatives—
  some proportion of the 48 percent of those voting in House
  elections in 1994 who cast their votes for Democrats
- As many poor whites as can be persuaded, for reasons of
  economic interest, to cooperate politically across racial lines
- Some of those millions of Americans of all races who no

longer take part in the two-party system or in politics at all, nonvoters whose active participation could change the face of American politics

Halfway through the twenty-first century, the U.S. population will be about evenly divided: between non-Hispanic whites and the so-called minority groups. The Census Bureau estimates that in the relatively near future 40 million Asians, 60 million blacks (compared with 30 million today), and 80 million Hispanics will be living in America. California and Texas, two of the three largest states, soon will have white *minorities*. Already, in California, blacks are a smaller group than Hispanics or Asians; in less than twenty years, Hispanics will be the largest "minority" in the nation.

The overall minority population will have *quadrupled*. And by 2050 Americans will number 392 million of all races, 52 percent more than the 259 million we are today (most living in already overcrowded cities). There's no reason to suppose that all these added millions, even the non-Hispanic whites, will be conservatives on today's model—at least not if there's a plausible alternative.

It's certainly to be hoped, on the other hand, that not all these new Americans will be living in poverty; but if present trends don't change, many *will* be poor and ill educated—which, for the future, presupposes low-income status. But not all of even those will necessarily be sympathetic to liberal programs or radical economic proposals.

Still, the potential seems to exist for a third party to tap into a swiftly rising population likely to encounter some degree of economic and racial disadvantage, hence to be anxious for economic change. For that prospect to materialize, often jealous or hostile "minorities" would have to be brought into political cooperation. Another daunting task would be to overcome the demonstrated reluctance of poor whites—in the old South or today's cities—to cross deeply entrenched racial lines to make common cause with African-Americans.

In the few decades of racial integration and backlash, no one has felt more threatened than low-income whites, often members of ethnic groups quartered together in jealously guarded neighborhoods and themselves insecure in their jobs and social status, particularly in an unstable economy. Affirmative action, antidiscrimination laws in housing, busing, school desegregation—all have seemed to many poor whites to be efforts by the larger society to force black gains at *their* expense. And blacks have often responded with angry attitudes toward "crackers" and "rednecks."

Nevertheless, the common problems of poor whites and blacks (and other minorities too) persist: joblessness, inadequate education, little or no health care, substandard nutrition and housing, indifferent police protection. These common problems create common interests, despite divisive racial animosities, and these interests become more compelling every year.

An effective new-party strategy therefore would emphasize these common interests—something neither mainstream party is willing to do—and seek changes in economic and social policies damaging to poor blacks *and* poor whites. In the last two decades, at the presidential campaign level, only Jesse Jackson has discussed such commonality of interests:

> We lost 800,000 family farms in the 1980s. Those farms didn't go from white to black. We lost thousands of manufacturing jobs in the 1980s. Those jobs didn't go from white to black. There are 40 million Americans that have no health plan, many don't have insurance. There are another 40 million that have inadequate health insurance. Of the 40 million in poverty, about 29 million are whites. The poor are mostly white, female and young.... When I march with mine workers in Bigstone Gap, Virginia, they are mostly white mine workers. When I march with machinists in Seattle ... when I march with family farmers in Iowa, they are mostly white.... [1]

As for the nonvoters, their political potential is unlimited but hard to develop. The 1994 elections were hailed by the Committee for the Study of the American Electorate for a relatively high turnout in a nonpresidential election. Yet only 38.7 percent of those eligible to vote, in one of the bitterest and most publicized campaigns in years, were moved to do so.

At that, the national turnout percentage got a boost from the close North-Robb senatorial campaign in Virginia, a race that brought out an enormous 16.4-point increase in voter participation over that of the 1990 midterm election. Still, the total Virginia turnout was just under 41 percent of those eligible to vote. Nationally about 75 million Americans cast ballots; an estimated 112.4 million stayed home.

Since 1962 not once have as many as half of those eligible to vote done so in a nonpresidential election. The highest national turnout was 48.6 percent in 1966, as the Republicans sought survival and the white backlash gained momentum. In 1994 the highest turnout in any state was the 59.6 percent recorded in South Dakota. But even that meant that 40 percent of South Dakotans did not choose to vote, and in all other states, the record was worse.

Not many more Americans nationwide cast a ballot even when the presidency is at stake. The hard-fought Nixon-Kennedy campaign of 1960, featuring two passionately supported candidates running in a virtual dead heat, was the last in which as much as 60 percent of the electorate went to the polls. In most presidential years since, little more than 50 percent of those eligible have voted.

That's the sorry story of those eligible and registered to vote. Millions more voting-age Americans are not registered and evince no interest whatever in the nation's politics. The reasons for such apathy are hotly debated and highly speculative, but more and more analysts are concurring, these days, with Curtis Gans, the director of the Committee for the Study of the American Electorate: "The sad fact of our political life is that the combination of perceived ineffective government and corrosive and vacuous elections is destroying both the citizenry's will to participate and its faith in the utility of our political institutions and the political process itself."[2]

That may be true of many African-Americans who can see

that politicians generally are more interested in appeals to the white middle class than to the black community. Some substantial percentage of today's nonvoters probably consists also of those Americans shown by the *Statistical Abstract of the United States* for 1994 to have been living in poverty in 1992: 24.5 million whites (11.6 percent of all whites), 10.6 million blacks (33.3 percent of all blacks), and 6.7 million Hispanics (29.3 percent of all Hispanics). That's 41.8 million Americans (14.5 percent of the total) living in poverty.

Many of these poor Americans see no reason to take part in a political system they believe has no interest in and never benefits them, in which they therefore feel they have no real stake and in which they can observe far more effort and concern being devoted to the rich and to the middle class. A political bonanza surely awaits the party or candidate or theme (or any combination thereof) that can lure a significant percentage of nonvoters, particularly the poor and alienated, to the polls.

An important step toward that goal would be black separation from a Democratic party that does not truly have at heart the interests of African-Americans or the nonblack poor. Such a breakaway would provide a base and a platform and could lead to formation of a more broadly based political party working for racial integration, economic opportunity for all poor Americans, and an equal place for them in American life.

By racial integration I don't mean a black-white amalgamation in which all ethnic and economic distinctions would be extinguished. I certainly do not mean the smothering of a distinctive and valuable black culture and its absorption into some misconceived melting pot. I am not even referring to a "color-blind society" in any sense except one in which all races have equal, and equally observed, legal rights.

Racial integration means to me, rather, a situation in which blacks and whites live together in amity, respecting each other's rights and culture, in a society in which neither can or needs to look down on faces permanently at the bottom of the well, a society in which neither race is threatened by the other nor has to claim preferential treatment in order to thrive economically.

Applied to racial relations in America in the last decade of the twentieth century, that description fails in every particular. While a relatively few blacks and whites (mostly at moderate to high income levels) do live together in amity, respecting each other's rights, relations between whites and African-Americans are generally distant and often hostile; nor are any of those other criteria widely met. In particular, as will be argued in more detail in Chapters Seven and Eight, whites for years have enjoyed preferential treatment, and many African-Americans as a consequence of centuries of deprivation and disdain temporarily need such treatment still if they are to meet educational and economic standards set by more fortunate whites. Democrats as well as Republicans, however, are backing away from affirmative action for blacks or anything smacking of the kind of racial preference that whites once took for granted for themselves.

In fact, the kind of integrated society described above is not likely to be achieved or even sought by mainstream parties that follow rather than lead social trends in a population that for years has been turning its back on racial integration. Historically the political center has controlled mainstream political parties, whether Democratic or Republican, though in recent years the right, in some cases the far right, has gained greater influence within Republican councils. But neither the center nor the right will urge, much less carry out, the kind of economic reform poor African-Americans and poor whites alike need if they are ever to approach economic equality and social justice in America.

When the supposedly liberal Democrats dominated Congress, they carefully avoided pushing for such reforms. But by openly preaching their own values, the Republicans made the Democrats seem more liberal than they actually were and persuaded Americans that conservative Republicans were more to be trusted with the powers of government. More important, both Republicans and Democrats owe allegiance to financially supportive, aggressively conservative business interests. Consequently both parties in recent decades have been instruments of the status quo, not of change, certainly not of radical change.

Even the program of today's Gingrich Republicans, if carried out, would move the nation away from its post–New Deal Democratic course only to the pre-New Deal center. Gingrich and his party are not challenging the political dominance of the center—their program is designed to appeal to it—and will make only cosmetic changes, if any, in the way corporations influence the economy and the parties.

The electoral college, too, tends toward stability, not change. Every four years it responds to the great, inclusive center, not to the ideological splinter. Such groups' popular support, though it may be considerable, usually has not translated into the electoral votes required by the Constitution for the election of a president. The Founders planned it that way.

Few African-Americans, however, are part of the stable center; most have instead a profound need to work toward greater social and economic equality. It's familiarly argued—particularly by white Democrats who need black votes—that only major parties can win national power and that therefore African-American interests are best served by continued black loyalty to the modern Democratic party. Black voters help the Democrats win elections—sometimes, anyway—and the Democrats claim to be more sympathetic to African-American interests than are the Republicans.

That's the same old argument the Republicans used to make when African-Americans were loyal adherents to *their* party, the party of Lincoln.

For nearly three quarters of a century after emancipation, in fact, blacks (the relative few who were allowed to vote) were all but unanimously Republican. Their loyalty was underwritten by Republican patronage in the South, where most blacks then lived.

In Hamlet, North Carolina, where I grew up in the 1930s and 1940s, white people thought it funny, typical of inept blacks, that the only registered black voter in town, the black high school principal, was one of the few Republicans. Sometimes the joke was told the other way around: A Republican was the only black voter.

Before 1932 Republicans usually could take black support as much for granted as Democrats now do, and they usually did. Hundreds, perhaps thousands of blacks were lynched in the United States in the late nineteenth and early twentieth centuries,* but the Republican presidents of that era took little, if any, notice and less action. Woodrow Wilson, the southern-born Democratic nominee in the three-way election of 1912, saw that blacks were in much the same political quandary as they are today: Their chosen party was not doing much for them, other than for patronage in the South. Wilson seized the moment and expressed his "earnest wish to see justice done to the colored people in every matter" and solemnly promised "absolute fair dealing."

Perhaps one hundred thousand northern blacks, including W.E.B. Du Bois, spurned President William H. Taft and former President Theodore Roosevelt, the Republican and Progressive nominees, to help put Wilson, the Democrat, in the White House. In the long American tradition he did not come through for them as promised, even permitting the further segregation of the Post Office and Treasury departments.[3]

As one result, blacks remained mostly Republican for another quarter century. Then, in the thirties, the Depression, the economic promise of Franklin Roosevelt's New Deal, Eleanor Roosevelt's dedicated advocacy of their concerns, and FDR's Executive Order 8802, barring racial discrimination in defense industries and the federal government,[†] converted blacks en masse. Their new allegiance to the Democrats—only briefly interrupted by their substantial support for Dwight Eisenhower—

---

*W.E.B. Du Bois estimated that seventeen hundred blacks were lynched in America in the decade 1885-94.

†Roosevelt's hand was forced by A. Philip Randolph, president of the Brotherhood of Sleeping Car Porters. Randolph threatened to lead a hundred thousand black demonstrators in a march on Washington if the president did not sign the order.

was cemented by the desegregation of the armed forces and by civil rights legislation pushed by nonsouthern Democrats in the administrations of Truman, Kennedy, and Johnson.

As integration faltered and the backlash mounted, however, both parties began to flee from economic reform and to allow the race question in national party politics to be addressed mostly in hostile terms. Beginning in 1968 and in every election since, owing to Democratic caution or default, the Republicans have been permitted to define racial issues. They did it usually by focusing on and denigrating what they described as black behavior—out-of-wedlock births, crime, welfare—in order to win white political support. Little attention was paid by either party to blacks' economic needs or, in consequence, to those similar needs of poor whites. As a predictable result, whites mostly voted Republican, blacks stayed largely with the less hostile Democrats, and the poor of both races stayed poor or got poorer.

Black support for Democrats in these years has been paradoxical, however, because *the Democrats consistently lost presidential elections*—not least because African-Americans and Democrats were so closely identified with each other. The Democratic party, after 1964, lost a critical and growing share of the white vote* owing to the party's supposed devotion to black interests.

Sometime in the late eighties, for example, when I was covering the Senate campaign of William Winter, a white Democrat and a distinguished former governor of Mississippi, I followed him to a Democratic party precinct meeting in the northern part of his state. All those in attendance were African-Americans, clear testament to white flight from the local Democratic party and clear evidence that Bill Winter was going to lose. He did, to Trent Lott, a white Republican, now the assistant Senate majority leader.

Recognizing the problem, white Democrats have sought to "move to the center" (which in most cases meant moving to

---

*The last Democratic presidential candidate to carry a majority of the nation's white males—who cast a massive number of votes—was Lyndon B. Johnson in 1964.

the right), trying to suppress race as an issue and to disguise, if not deny, their long association with blacks. That brought about a new Democratic emphasis on issues the Republicans already had preempted—the "middle class," tax cuts, crime, and the like. Blacks loyal to the Democrats had little choice but to go along with this deemphasis of *their* interests.

Even this copycat strategy did not work nationally until 1992, when a lagging economy, George Bush's ineptitude, and Ross Perot's weird candidacy helped put Bill Clinton in the White House—just barely, with 43 percent of the popular vote.

By then, both parties had effectively abandoned integration as a national policy, beyond what already had been achieved, and even that much was coming under fire.

Neither party was pressing hard for further racial gains or enforcement of what had been done, and both treated racial aspirations largely as a patronage problem to be handled by Cabinet appointments and other political spoils. Most important, neither party was willing or professed to see the necessity to mount an attack on the economic problems that had created the inner-city ghetto and that were also keeping many whites in poverty and hopelessness.

Thus today's uneasy alliance between African-Americans and the Democratic party of Bill Clinton is a world apart from the sixties coalition of nonsouthern Democrats and the civil rights movement. Then a realizable goal—desegregation in the South—was shared on both sides of the coalition. John F. and Robert Kennedy, their hands forced by the civil rights movement and segregationist stupidities, reluctantly accepted that goal and furthered it.

Later it seemed momentarily possible that Lyndon Johnson might lead the nation to real integration; then he began futilely to pursue a "bitch of a war," as he called it, on the other side of the world.[4] In retrospect, even the hard-driving Johnson probably could not have overcome the innate antiblack prejudice that began showing itself again in white America in the late sixties.

Today, despite blacks' general belief that Democrats are marginally preferable to Republicans, the alliance stands for no specific goal and for little of real benefit to African-Americans:

Does it promise an attack on the ills of the inner-city ghetto?

Clinton barely mentioned those ills in his campaign, and when he later spoke out at Memphis against black crime, he only demanded poor blacks' moral self-improvement. In 1994 he decided that he could not risk tax increases to pay for the alternatives to welfare he had proposed in his campaign—job training, for instance, and support for two-earner families nearing poverty. Welfare opponents promptly began preparing to carry out the *other* and more punitive part of Clinton's campaign promise: to cut off welfare benefits after a recipient had been on the rolls for two years. By late 1995, the president was complaining that his own welfare proposals had been "too weak," and saying that he would sign a Senate version of a punitive bill that would consign perhaps a million more children to poverty and provide several billion less for child care than he had proposed. Perhaps worse, the bill would end the federal commitment to welfare, a commitment dating back to the 1930s.

Clinton protested only feebly, if at all, as the Federal Reserve, ever in pursuit of inflation, raised interest rates to a point that slowed recovery from the early-nineties recession. And why should African-Americans support a president who gave such high priority and strong backing to a crime bill featuring death penalties for a new group of crimes, more prisons to incarcerate more blacks, more police rather than more economic opportunity, and a punitive public relations ploy called "three strikes and you're out"?*

---

*The tough-sounding three-strike provision would imprison an offender for life after conviction for a third felony. In Washington, the only state with such a law in 1994, it also had caused criminals to resist arrest and had inhibited plea bargaining, thus endangering police officers and cluttering already overcrowded courts. Convicted third-strike offenders, knowing they were in for life, became more dangerous to prison guards and other inmates. And costly life terms for relatively minor crimes eventually would expand the need to build more expensive prison cells.

Does black support for the Democratic party produce changes in established economic approaches, with the aim of redressing glaring racial and class inequities?

Clinton's short-lived effort to stimulate the economy early in his term was watered down by both parties in Congress to little more than mush. His deficit reduction policies, which actually produced deficit reduction in his first two years, were conventional and conservative in deference to "the market"; after the 1994 elections he hastily dealt himself into the Republicans' tax-cutting game, and his 1995 budget seemed to abandon deficit reduction without seeking fundamental economic change. His health care proposals carefully bowed to the insurance companies and went nowhere in 1993 and 1994. Neither he nor any leading Democrat has put forward an economic idea more radical than Republican Jack Kemp's flawed enterprise zones proposal or as radical as the Family Assistance Plan, the guaranteed annual income sponsored by Richard Nixon twenty years ago.

No wonder, then, that after the Democrats' 1994 election debacle, when Secretary of Commerce Ron Brown asked a group of black activists, "How do we reelect Bill Clinton?" one of his hearers answered in effect: "Why should we?"[5]

Why indeed? The record shows that both established political parties and their leaders (the Republicans more candidly) have failed to address the deepest needs of African-Americans and of the poor generally—more than forty million Americans. Instead they have presided over years of grudging desegregation followed by widespread backlash and continuing discrimination; white and corporate blindness to blacks' and poor whites' economic disadvantages; inequitable tax policies; a deteriorating wage structure; black political empowerment largely unable to pursue basic black interests through mainstream politics; underclass growth, increased crime, and rising fear of crime; white flight from a decaying public school system and white abandonment of the inner city; the decline and only partial recovery of the manufacturing sector, the increasing use throughout the economy of part-time rather than fully employed workers, and the massive layoffs of working Americans, black and white, by hugely profitable companies and their highly paid executives.

No African-American should be embarrassed, much less feel disloyal, in deciding to turn away from such a record and from the mainstream parties that compiled it.

4 Liberal vs. Conservative

We [blacks] need to start thinking of ourselves instead of falling on the knife for the Democrats every election and getting nothing for it.

Professor Robert Starks,
Northeastern Illinois University[1]

At the height of the 1994 campaign the Republican polltaker Frank Luntz inquired plaintively of his party: "Why are we taking each other down? It's almost as if we had a death wish."

At the time Luntz seemed to have good reason for his question. Republican Senator John Warner of Virginia had declared Republican nominee Oliver North unfit for the state's other Senate seat. Former President Reagan's wife had blasted North as a liar. The Republican mayors of the nation's two largest cities opposed party nominees, Rudolph Giuliani of New York endorsing Democrat Mario Cuomo for governor, Richard Riordan of Los Angeles supporting Democrat Dianne Feinstein for the Senate. William Bennett and Jack Kemp, both former Republican Cabinet officers, repudiated Proposition 187, the anti-immigration ballot initiative in California that was supported by Republican Governor Pete Wilson and Republican Senate candidate Michael Huffington.

On the Democratic side, candidates in droves (including the

Speaker of the House, Tom Foley, whose district defeated him) turned their backs on President Clinton, either avoiding his campaign help or opposing various aspects of his program. And no sooner had returns announced a Republican triumph than Senator Richard Shelby of Alabama, a Democrat who had often voted like a Republican, jumped formally to the GOP, a fine example of opportunism and ideology embracing.

Immediate political reasons for these defections were obvious. Perhaps more ominous for the Democrats was an early-1995 report by Robert Novak—a conservative commentator but an astute political reporter—that Democratic members of the House had found their leadership uninspired during a party retreat at Piney Point, Maryland. Fewer than half the 203 House Democrats had even attended, and a "mainstream liberal" told Novak that the gathering reminded him of the last days of the Communist party in the old Soviet Union: "The apparatus was there, the hierarchy, the organization. But all of a sudden, the party was gone—just like that. I get the same feelings about the Democratic party today."[2]

This gloomy report, the 1994 defections, the enthusiasm for Ross Perot's ill-defined presidential candidacy, and other less-publicized developments suggest a rising restiveness among candidates, officeholders, and voters alike with the limitations and liabilities of being Republican or—perhaps particularly—Democrat or having to make the choice between only those two.

In August 1995, for example, Bill Bradley of New Jersey, one of the best minds among Democratic leaders, announced his retirement from the U.S. Senate. He did not repudiate speculation that he might be an independent or third-party candidate for president in 1996. Perot, too, allowed talk of another presidential candidacy to flourish. At about the same time, following publication of a new book by Colin Powell, he too became the subject of much talk about a possible presidential bid, either as a Republican or a non–major party candidate.

In that same month the Times Mirror Center for the People

and the Press found in a nationwide poll that 26 percent of 1,476 respondents would welcome an independent presidential candidate in 1999. An unnamed Republican was favored by 35 percent and the reelection of Democrat Bill Clinton by 32 percent. These results were not far from a three-way split, and support for an independent had increased for the third time in eight months.

New laws, moreover, make the major parties no longer a prime source of funds for candidates. The party "image" is not always vital to them in modern times and can be damaging. Bradley attacked both parties for a lack of vision and relevance to the national needs. Television, more than party, now yields personal and political identification, but TV campaigning costs big money—particularly in large jurisdictions like California—and candidates, not the party, must raise most of it themselves.

Television therefore has eroded party loyalty and the power of appeals to that loyalty. To the extent that TV exposure can be bought and paid for, moreover, the prospects for a new party or an independent candidacy can be quickly improved by an expensive but effective television campaign. Perot's relative success in 1992 is inconceivable without his TV appearances, free or purchased.

For all these reasons, modern political parties have less cohesiveness and power than they had years ago. That's why Republicans and some Democrats run more nearly as "conservatives" than under their party label. That's why independent candidacies at the state level multiplied and had some success in 1994, and probably will again in 1996 and later. No doubt that's why even the erratic Perot, running as an independent, dropping out and coming in again, polled nearly 20 percent of the presidential vote in 1992, and why Bradley would even consider an independent run in 1996. Voters today are looking for other choices than the limited one they perceive between Democrats and Republicans, candidates everywhere are willing, even eager to offer those other choices, and TV provides the instrument.

The political suicide Frank Luntz feared did not, of course, materialize for the Republicans in 1994. Among other developments, their electoral successes were a practical disaster for black representation in Congress, as well as a general rebuff to black concerns. The Black Caucus in the House now is part of the minority, faces an unsympathetic majority, and, with other special-interest caucuses, is no longer funded by public money. Most caucus members were reelected, but in the present Congress they have had to relinquish three committee chairmanships, seventeen subcommittee chairmanships, and the accompanying staff resources—a substantial blow.

Other stresses are affecting the Democratic-black alliance. Many knowledgeable African-Americans have come to believe in recent years that Democratic support for civil rights three decades ago may have been calculated as much to win votes for the party in the big black communities then new and growing in northern and western cities as to improve the lives and situations of African-Americans. Blacks have ample reason to question too whether Democrats are more concerned with recapturing a big share of the white southern and white male vote—lost, since the sixties, to the backlash—than with furthering the interests of African-Americans.

African-Americans are not blind. They see both parties exploiting white racial attitudes for political advantage: patrician George Bush in 1988 with the Willie Horton television commercials, good ole boy Bill Clinton in 1992 with studied criticism of the black rap singer Sister Souljah, as well as distant relations with Jesse Jackson. African-Americans are not unaware, moreover, that three times as many blacks as whites were living in poverty in 1959 and that despite their consistent support for the Democrats since the New Deal, three times as many blacks as whites *still* were living in poverty in 1989.

With the once-clear and common target of segregation in the South a thing of the past, with white animosity and fear of blacks increasing, it seems entirely plausible to skeptical African-Americans that the Democratic party today counts on the support of black voters, believing they have "nowhere else to go," without trying to deliver much in return.

"After the civil rights movement, we thought we had won the war," Robert Starks, a political scientist at Northeastern Illinois University, recalled in 1994. "But to whites it was simply a skirmish. Whites are saying, 'Sure, you won the Battles of the Sixties, but we won the war.' "[3]

White Democrats cannot, however, complacently rely on the notion that African-Americans have nowhere else to go. A wholesale black flight to the Republicans probably is not in the cards, though the GOP is making marginal gains in the few areas where it has made blacks feel welcome.

Even in the conservative tide of 1994 Republican Governors Pete Wilson of California and John Engler of Michigan each got 13 percent of the black vote. New York's Democratic senator, Daniel P. Moynihan, lost 20 percent of black votes in the general election, after defeating the African-American Al Sharpton in a primary.

Nevertheless, only 9 percent of voting blacks went Republican in all of 1994's House races. If, however, even a relatively small percentage of black voters in any given election should decide to "take a walk" and vote for neither party, dropping their support for a Democratic candidate from the usual 85 or 95 percent to, say, 65 or 75 percent, that Democrat would be in serious trouble.

Something like that may have hurt Governor Mario Cuomo of New York, a Democrat who lost his 1994 campaign for a fourth term by only about two hundred thousand votes. He got 88 percent of black votes statewide, but a year earlier David Dinkins had won 95 percent in the New York City mayoralty race. Cuomo's campaign strategists had refused to put up, until too late, the money to finance a get out the vote drive in state assembly districts represented by African-American legislators.

In 1985, 60 percent of New Jersey black voters opted *for* the incumbent "liberal Republican" governor Tom Kean, who easily won reelection. In 1993 black voters in Virginia, perhaps affected by the fact that the African-American Douglas Wilder was in-eligible constitutionally for a second term, turned out in lower numbers than they had for Wilder four years earlier. Partially as a result, George Allen, a white Republican, was elected. Conversely, a heavy turnout of Virginia blacks helped defeat Oliver North, the white Republican Senate candidate in 1994.

Relatively low black voter turnout in the 1993 New Jersey gubernatorial election fatally damaged Democrat Jim Florio's re-election effort. Christine Whitman, the Republican challenger, campaigned more in the image of Tom Kean and Dwight Eisenhower than that of Ronald Reagan, and New Jersey blacks believed Florio had taken their support too much for granted, as many African-Americans believe the national Democratic party does. Black voting declined by 25 percent statewide and by varying percentages in urban, heavily Democratic, heavily black Essex and Hudson counties. That defection from Florio, despite his good record on racial issues, was a major factor in the governor's unexpected defeat.*

Thus the latent power of black voters to affect the outcome of elections, if not to win them for one of their own, is evident. That illustrates the danger to Democrats of depending so heavily on African-American votes, possibly someday to a Democratic presidential candidate. Unlikely? Perhaps, but the unlikely often happens in politics.

Suppose the Democratic presidential nominee was Sam Nunn of Georgia;† suppose that his opponent was a relatively liberal Republican like William Weld of Massachusetts or even someone more conservative, with Weld or Christine Whitman on the Republican ticket as the vice presidential nominee. In such an event blacks might move in considerable numbers to the Republicans; or if they merely failed to turn out a big vote for Nunn, he could lose.

Or suppose Bill Bradley wages an independent or third-party presidential campaign in 1996. Many blacks undoubtedly would support him, owing to his outstanding record on racial issues.

---

*A bigger share of black voters for a Republican candidate usually results from a drop in black turnout. Black Republicans, like white Republicans, are more apt to vote than Democrats.
†Nunn has announced that he will not seek reelection to the Senate, but could still be a future presidential candidate.

That could mean defeat for Bill Clinton, the likely Democratic nominee, even if Bradley did not actually win the presidency.

Roger Wilkins, the former assistant attorney general in the Kennedy-Johnson Justice Department, now a history professor at George Mason University in Virginia, recalls attending a party at which other blacks excitedly discussed the possibility that the African-American general Colin Powell might run for president in 1996. When Wilkins asked what if Powell were the Republican *vice presidential nominee* on a ticket headed by former Vice President Dan Quayle, a prominent African-American Democrat responded: "In a minute, I'd vote for them."[4]

That doesn't necessarily mean that all or even most African-Americans would support such a ticket. But there's little doubt that racial solidarity, General Powell's experience, his high stature as a black "role model," and his lack (so far) of political liabilities would make any ticket that included him attractive to the black community. If a Republican presidential nominee more nearly acceptable to African-Americans than Dan Quayle*—say, Lamar Alexander, the former governor of Tennessee, or even Senator Bob Dole of Kansas—were to choose General Powell as his running mate in 1996, Powell's strong appeal to blacks might make that ticket a winner.

There's no doubt that if in the future one of the mainstream parties nominated the general for president, he would quickly achieve something near unanimous African-American support. The nomination of an African-American for president by a major party would be a breakthrough of enormous consequence for the black community—and for whites too: another taboo down the drain, another long step toward national inclusion.

Whether an African-American in today's antiblack climate actually could be elected president obviously is another question.

In a recent survey of 1,206 randomly selected African-

---

*Quayle has announced that he will not seek the presidency in 1996 but has not ruled out a future candidacy. Though Powell too has declined a 1996 presidential candidacy, the number two spot on the Republican ticket remains a live possibility for him.

Americans, Michael Dawson of the University of Chicago and Ronald Brown of Wayne State University found fully half favoring formation of a black third party. Almost 8 in 10 said the American economic and legal systems were unfair to blacks; 7 in 10 thought that in predominantly black communities blacks should control the government and the economy.

The survey also noted "the emergence of a generation gap," with black nationalist sentiment strongest among African-Americans in their mid-thirties and younger. These African-Americans generally had been too young to experience the civil rights movement's successes in the late fifties and the sixties; they had seen instead the backlash of the seventies and eighties.[5]

Roger Wilkins, in many talks with black students, also has noticed what he calls their "dissociation" from the older "civil rights generation"—a collective lack of memory of civil rights gains and a sense that in their lifetimes white society has done little to improve the economic and social lot of the black community, sometimes even opposing steps that might bring improvement.[6] That sounds suspiciously like "dissociation" also from the Democrats.

Such a generational division among African-Americans suggests, of course, that a complete switchover from the Democratic to a new party is not likely in any foreseeable circumstance. But it also could mean diminishing black support for the Democrats. The interest in a new political movement shown by a rising generation of African-Americans, dissatisfied with the present, unbeholden to the past, seems to improve the outlook for a new party, even if at first it might split the black vote.

On the other hand, the fact that most black political leaders—say, John Conyers of Michigan or Charles Rangel of New York—are older and are committed Democrats, with much to lose by leaving the party and much to preserve by staying with it, probably militates against the idea of a new party. So do the personal interests of those thousands of black Democrats who are elected officials in various localities.

*   *   *

Traditionalists will argue, as I have in other circumstances, that third parties and independent candidacies never seem to break the hold of the two-party system on American voters; witness, most recently, the rise and fall and limited rerise of Ross Perot in 1992. This traditional argument is underpinned, and powerfully, by the history of third parties' failures to win office or to survive in what was once the tightly constrained world of centrist American politics.

In this century substantial but still splinter political movements have been led by Theodore Roosevelt, Robert M. La Follette, Strom Thurmond, Henry Wallace, George Wallace, John Anderson, and Ross Perot. The campaign of the last, however, may have been groundbreaking in a new era of television politics and voter volatility. A big-eared, wisecracking Texas businessman with plenty of money and no political record, Perot first entered the presidential race on a television talk show, then dropped out with an implausible excuse, and finally came in again, ostensibly at the behest of "volunteers" but just in time to take part in televised presidential debates. If he could win a fifth of the vote against the mainstream candidates, perhaps someone more glamorous, steadfast, experienced and focused—also, of course, with plenty of money—might do even better in 1996, particularly if Newt Gingrich's Republicans have disappointed the public.

Besides, the historical evidence of third parties' electoral failures ignores the profound effect they often have had on the other two parties, hence on American politics, by the forces third-party efforts mobilized and by later Democratic or Republican efforts to win back third-party bolters. Perot voters, perhaps the vanguard of contemporary revolt against the two-party system, went heavily Republican in 1994, a major reason for that party's victory and strong evidence of President Clinton's failure to satisfy 1992's most obvious dissidents.

Evidence of this function of a third party or an independent was most graphically provided by George Wallace. His backlash, anti-integration presidential campaigns and his personal magnetism galvanized millions of disgruntled white voters. Though he never won and probably never could have won the presidency, he changed the faces of the two mainstream parties, was a powerful factor in the nation's retreat from integration, and both foreshadowed and facilitated the coming of Ronald Reagan.

The argument that third parties never win also overlooks one great success, the Republicans. Founded in the 1850s out of frustration with the failure of the then-established Democrats and Whigs to cope with the national crisis over chattel slavery in the South, the Republicans first contended for the presidency in 1856. Failing then, even in a weakened two-party system, the new party, helped by continuing crisis, held together, gained strength as the Whigs withered away, and won in 1860 with former Whig Abraham Lincoln as its presidential nominee.

Lincoln won primarily because the Democrats, under the pressures of the slavery struggle, split into three factions, allowing him to slip into the White House with only 37 percent of the popular vote but a majority in the electoral college. Lincoln's election on a "Radical Republican" platform precipitated southern secession and the Civil War, but his successful prosecution of that war and preservation of the Union established the Republicans as a major political party, dominant for the rest of the nineteenth and into the early twentieth century and returning to such dominance in the last years of this century.

Nothing as openly threatening as the breakup of the Union now confronts Americans. But if contemporary Democrats and Republicans do not face up to the failure of integration and to the glaring economic inequities that afflict so many Americans of both races, a new party to confront a different kind of crisis soon may prove as necessary as one was in the 1850s.

Conservatives' seizure of power *within* the Republican party in the early sixties is another example of successful breakaway action. Though it did not lead to formation of an officially new party, it *did* lead to the presidential nomination of Barry Goldwater in 1964 and to his party's jettisoning of the moderate "me too" racial and economic policies espoused by Dwight Eisenhower and his followers.

That conservative coup and George Wallace's national campaigns produced the great transformation from the New Deal era to the age of conservatism and to the twenty years in which Richard Nixon, Gerald Ford, Ronald Reagan, and George Bush wielded power from the White House. This political transformation moved even the Democratic administrations of Jimmy Carter and Bill Clinton, as well as the Democratic party itself, to the right. Ultimately it produced the triumph of Newt Gingrich, however ephemeral that may prove.

The Republicans, save a few holdouts like Senators John Chaffee of Rhode Island and Mark Hatfield of Oregon, already have become an all-but-official Conservative party. That can be counterbalanced only by an equally official and dedicated Liberal party.

As a political commentator I consistently opposed such divisions, believing instead that two inclusive, nonideological parties were more appropriate to a federal system of government. I thought that the two-party system enhanced necessary stability and eased transfers of power between parties, and I feared that minor but passionate doctrinal disputes might further splinter ideological parties into numerous small factions like those that dominate some European nations.

In recent years, moreover, it's appeared likely that the conservatives might always win in an ideologically divided society, just as, decades ago, Democrats and liberals seemed likely to be perpetually in power.

Now, however, the labels "Democrat" and "Republican" have lost much of their persuasive power. More and more voters appear to want some other kind of choice; conservative or liberal seems their preference. Though conservatives now are winning, that need not continue to be so, particularly if the Gingrich-led Republican Congress tries to return the nation to a pre–New Deal stage, as it apparently intends. And an ideologically liberal party—by which I mean one truly committed, not just paying lip service, to economic opportunity and social justice for all— might find a greater audience if its leaders openly asserted its values and ideals.

No Democratic party leader has done that since Lyndon Johnson, and he not only was mistrusted as a "wheeler-dealer" but dissipated his credibility in Vietnam. President Clinton has focused on the middle class. Democratic party and congressional leaders, since liberalism has come under such severe attack, have tended at best to be "closet liberals," not standing forthrightly for liberal ideas but diluting and attempting to conceal, even deny liberal approaches.

As has been the way of American politics, a new political party will not materialize overnight—complete, tidy, tightly organized, with a ten-point program—or as a result of academic conferences. Politics seldom works so neatly; Franklin Roosevelt, for example, won election in the dark days of 1932 on the slogan but not the specifics of the New Deal. FDR did not know himself all that he would try, what would fail, and what succeed.

So a new political party will emerge, if at all, probably messily, pragmatically, over time, in response to varying necessities, perhaps in the actions and ideas of one or more political campaigns, at the call of one or more candidates.

A new party, moreover, may never elect a president; no third party save the Republicans of 1860 ever has. That does not mean that none has *mattered*. A new party's ultimate importance could well be the classic consequence of third parties in America, the exertion of a powerful influence on the future of one or both of the mainstream parties. If so, it would achieve the *effect* of power, which sometimes is more useful than the *form* of power.

Change of New Deal magnitude, of course, is hard to conceive without a persuasive leader. American politics always has been deeply responsive to personality: Andrew Jackson, TR, John F. Kennedy. A new party leader with a scintillating personality and temperament, with the political instincts of a winner, who can be visualized as a winner, as were FDR and Ronald Reagan, would be a necessity. Sadly, no such leader is now in sight, certainly not within the bedraggled Democratic party; Bradley, for instance, is an impressive politician but scarcely a scintillating personality. Nor did one appear, even distantly, in the wreckage left to the party after the 1994 elections.

Colin Powell might well have been the right leader for the third party discussed here, although he is so far untested in a campaign. Powell has made it clear, however, that if he ever seeks the presidency, he will do so as a Republican.

In 1932, the FDR who was to bring the New Deal was not easily discernible in the governor of New York who sought the presidency so avidly. He was only a nice man who badly wanted to be president, wrote Walter Lippmann. Ronald Reagan in 1980 was an involuntarily retired movie actor who talked of "killer trees" and of whom the old Hollywood mogul Jack Warner, on hearing of Reagan's candidacy, had exclaimed: "No, no! James Stewart for President! Ronald Reagan for his best friend."

So who knows where or when or how another such "nice man" or "best friend," similarly ambitious and ready for leadership, might come forward? Lesser mortals, meanwhile, have the immediate and not less important task of giving purpose to a new party that might attract support from the growing populations of minorities, from those now too alienated from American society to vote, and from holdouts against the conservative tide. That purpose might well call forth a leader to champion it.

The program of such a party, most importantly, would promise *opportunity to the poor*, even to those presently lost souls in the inner city—not the opportunity to get rich or even necessarily to rise to the middle class, certainly not to eliminate all distinctions between rich and poor. It would offer only the opportunity to become useful, self-supporting, and respected citizens with a stake in community and country.

That opportunity—surely the minimum promise of America—is what is most grievously lacked by many African-Americans, many members of other minority groups, and millions of whites. It may not in every case be all that these Americans need in order to build better lives, and some probably would not have the ability to take advantage of it. They deserve the promise anyway; for the rest, that opportunity could open the door to a better future, hence a better nation for all.

A new party that offered such opportunity could have no greater mission and might find a passionate response. That mission could be defined and that response evoked by a pledge to work toward a policy of full employment at productive jobs for all Americans able and anxious to work.

5 Expanding the Center

We cannot . . . repair the American community
and restore the American family until we provide
the structure, the values, the discipline, and the
reward that work gives.

President Clinton

Nearly a quarter century ago Dr. Kenneth Clark wrote that
political activity—exercising the vote, seeking and holding
office—had replaced street demonstrations as "the new 'cutting
edge' of the civil rights movement."[1]

He and virtually all black leaders of the fifties and sixties and
Presidents Kennedy and Johnson, Nixon and Carter assumed
that if African-Americans were assured the vote and of their
right to hold public office, all else would follow. As a journalist
I shared that idea; full political citizenship for African-
Americans would make a reality of the ideals of economic and
social equality.

We were wrong. Over the last three decades much *has* been
accomplished within a newly active black political community.
Notably, blacks have been elected to important offices, and a
substantial black middle class, perhaps 40 percent of all African-
Americans, has developed.

Still, *political* power has not produced *economic* power, much less social equality for the great majority of African-Americans. Less than half the black community has achieved or held on to middle-class economic status, and the growth of the black middle class slowed almost to a standstill in the Reagan-dominated eighties. Few African-Americans who have "made it" to the middle class, certainly not those who haven't, would claim social standing and personal or professional respect equal to those of their white counterparts.

Terence O'Neill, an independent African-American architect in New York, for example, has been given responsibility for several large projects in Harlem. But he doesn't "get work below 96th Street or 110th Street." Another black architect, William E. Davis, Jr., concedes that race has affected his career too: "It's a subliminal thing that you're not qualified, even though all of us have gone to the same schools, have the same degrees and the same licenses. We [African-Americans] have to spend half the time proving that we're credible architects."[2]

Even black athletes, an elite cohort, have similar problems. Scott Galbraith, a tight end for the Dallas Cowboys, claims a "kinship" with the other Cowboys, black and white. But "when I go over to the mall, those aren't my teammates, those are white people. And I'm black." William Gaines, a defensive tackle for the Washington Redskins, has been stopped several times by police as he drove his pickup truck in suburban Virginia. And Ken Harvey, a Redskins linebacker, recalls: "I've had people follow me in stores and get nervous when you come on the elevator with them"[3]

Thus the early assumption of civil rights leaders and of liberals like me that black political empowerment would lead to other necessary gains for all blacks has proved unjustified. We underestimated, I believe, the long-term damage inflicted on African-Americans by centuries of blatant white supremacy; we did not sufficiently credit the persistence of the black poverty and disadvantage that resulted; above all, we too easily assumed that the innate white sense of superiority would fade as blacks voted.

It's plain now that those inner-city blacks noticed mostly when they appear on the nightly television news as perpetrators or victims of crime will be with us for years to come, a haunting, debilitating, accusative, often destructive presence in American life. Nor will most law-abiding, hardworking blacks in the lower economic groups soon rise to equality with most whites. The hard truth is that on the present political course economic power for most African-Americans will not be realized in the near future, if ever, and without general economic power, the black community can have little real political power.

In 1993, in a melancholy personal memoir, even Kenneth Clark, despairing at last of America's "deep and pervasive racism," concluded that "the methods of previous civil rights struggles have not redressed that racism. Even the increased number of black elected officials are unable to increase justice and humanity for those who have been forgotten in the inner cities. More appropriate and effective methods must now be developed. . . ."[4]

The idea was mistaken in the first place. Black empowerment within the white political mainstream never could have been the remedy for racial inequality. For one thing, economic studies show that political participation or the lack of it is not the most common denominator of poverty in America. Parental inheritance is: born poor, raised poor, likely to stay poor.

Even if relatively optimistic assumptions are made, for instance, the child of a father who is in the bottom 5 percent of income earners is about eight times likelier to remain poor or near poor than to rise to the top fifth. Conversely, most Americans born into the middle class or affluence stay in the same general income range.[5]

And in America, anyway, as events have convinced Henry Louis Gates of Harvard, "political power flows from economic power," not the other way around.[6] Few will doubt that who have seen the influence in Washington of great economic concentrations—say, the big agricultural interests—or who have studied the contribution lists of the political action committees that largely pay the huge costs of American politics and politicians.

With rare exceptions, those concentrations and those lists do not include African-Americans. It follows that African-Americans do not have much *real* political power, no matter how many mayors or city councillors they elect. Having little of the economic power that yields real political power, having failed to gain such economic power through mainstream electoral politics, and having little prospect of doing so in the future, African-Americans now face this daunting paradox: They must achieve the economic empowerment that leads to real political power through effective political action of their own, rather than in the white mainstream.

Then and only then might the controlling center of American politics expand to consider black interests equally with those of whites. Then and only then might African-Americans exert power in a much-expanded political center, on substantially equal terms with the whites who now dominate the smaller, existing political center.

African-Americans, in short, must build a new political party. The call to action would be sounded and the necessary political base provided by their declaration of independence from the Democratic party. The common interest around which cooperating groups might gather would be economic gain: gain for its own sake, gain for the greater political influence it would bring to the new party and its elements.

Economic gain is the first requisite if these groups are to seize and hold a more nearly equal place in American life. And that's why the first principle of a new party must be full employment.

Not much is heard about *that* these days, certainly not from the major political parties. The term has even gained a certain opprobrium. For one thing, many think of it falsely as "leaf raking," a sort of government-sponsored, taxpayer-financed haven of make-work jobs for those who won't or can't find employment in the private sector. For another, economists have associated the idea of full employment with inflation.

In the sixties it was believed that "full employment" had been effectively reached when unemployment was reduced to about 3 percent of the work force. That was considered a sort of irreducible minimum, owing to people who were changing jobs, to temporary and seasonal layoffs, and to the fear that if unemployment fell to an even lower level, competition for scarce labor would stimulate inflation.

It's a sad measure of what's happened in the intervening years that the irreducible minimum has been doubled, so that *6 percent* unemployment (meaning about nine million people officially out of work) is considered "full employment" today. And that figure doesn't include the millions of other Americans so discouraged or ill or disadvantaged that they have stopped looking for work and have dropped out of the work force altogether. These are not considered "officially" unemployed because they can't be counted as part of the labor force. Nevertheless, they are out of work, they don't get paid, sometimes they don't eat, and they have little hope for anything better.

Blacks, last hired and first fired, usually less qualified by education and training, have been the primary, though by no means the only, losers in the increased modern tolerance for joblessness. Indeed, millions more whites than blacks are officially and unofficially unemployed today (though white unemployment is not greater in proportion to population).

Real wages, meanwhile, have fallen steadily for those still working. That is a twenty-year trend, whether wages are measured hourly or weekly. In that period, only those earning more than $80,000 annually have managed to stay ahead of inflation. Those at the lower end of the wage spectrum actually lost ground to rising prices. Substantial growth of the workforce during the Clinton years has failed to change the wage trend and in some ways it has worsened.

For the year ending in September 1995—a year in which the economy expanded, the stock market boomed, and corporations reported strong profits—earnings for American workers rose by only 2.7 percent, the smallest increase on record, barely ahead of inflation, which ran at 2.5 percent during the same period. White-collar workers had slightly larger gains than blue-collar employees, and nonunion workers fared considerably better than union members. For years, new union contracts have resulted in smaller wage increases than the contracts they replaced.

Secretary of Labor Robert B. Reich, whose department reported these figures, seemed to understate the case when he said, "There is something wrong with rising profits, rising productivity and a soaring stock market but employee compensation heading nowhere."

The income and wealth gaps, as outlined earlier, have widened, with more rich people richer at the top and more poor people poorer at the bottom. Technology is replacing workers wholesale, highly profitable corporations are laying off personnel by the thousands, not to remain solvent but to reduce costs and increase profits, while temporary workers who do not rate perquisites like health insurance are being widely employed to replace once-regular employees now laid off.

In these circumstances a wage-push inflation seems a rather remote threat, hardly to be caused by expanding employment. And even the threat may be illusory: Between 1955 and 1965 wages rose 20 percent in real terms, but consumer prices increased only 1.6 percent a year. And unemployment was lower then than it is today.

Official unemployment dropped just below 6 percent in late 1994 (though it rose again in 1995). But in most recent years it has run regularly above that level—and just as regularly has been about twice as high for African-Americans as for whites. (For teenaged blacks, unemployment is off the charts.) Joblessness, affecting African-Americans disproportionately, is therefore a *racial* question, and since it has outsize impact on poor whites too, it's also a *class* issue.

More particularly, as suggested above, full employment would be the surest route to real political power, independent of white "concessions," for all African-Americans. Stable and productive jobs at decent pay for most African-American men and women would greatly increase blacks' political power, their standing in the overall community and in their own eyes, their hopes for "getting ahead" socially and economically, and—perhaps most important—their reason to believe themselves valuable and valued citizens.

A rising tide, as President Kennedy liked to say, lifts all boats. If economic opportunity and job security could be expanded in America, that would benefit not just African-Americans in particular but the working class in general. Economic gains for all— the expansion of the economic pie—would become the glue to hold together a new coalition of those once excluded from political power.

The expansion of the electorate by the civil rights gains of the sixties was accepted by whites as long as they did not consider themselves penalized or threatened. Whites were not, after all, losing their own votes; they were not even sacrificing much because in most cases they fully expected to, and did, remain in the dominant political majority.

As time passed, however, and regions other than the South began to feel themselves affected by the civil rights movement, whites, particularly low-income whites, began to resent economic devices like affirmative action that they saw as pitting blacks against whites. Putting a job, a contract, a promotion, or a school admission into the hands of an African-American seemed to be, and occasionally was, taking it out of the hands of a white, a matter of "their" gain, "our" loss.

So the central political strategy of a new party in the nineties and in the unaccountable century that looms beyond would be race-neutral, color-blind policies to expand the economic power of *all* poor Americans, who, of course, would include most African-Americans. This would not cause real sacrifices for most whites or erase basic economic differences between rich and poor or constitute a "redistribution" of wealth by government decree. It would narrow the income and wealth gaps but not eliminate them, and it might obliterate or obscure those faces at the bottom of the well.

Bill Clinton seemed to realize in 1992 that whites have shown themselves politically unwilling to accept economic and social losses for the sake of integration. Had he promised to raise taxes to invest in ghetto schools instead of pledging to "end welfare as we know it," he probably would not have been elected. Future presidential nominees of the mainstream parties will face the same dilemma; most will choose the same evasions.

Unemployment is not just a problem for African-Americans or even for all those without jobs. Thousands of black and white workers laid off from highly paid positions have gone back to work, mostly in the service sector, for far less than they once were paid. Such an economic comedown can drop a family out of the middle class into near-poverty and often means that youngsters cannot go on to higher education—an ill omen for the national future. Medical bills become disastrous; mortgage payments undertaken in better times can no longer be made; a wife may have to go to work and leave children untended.

The *fear* of being laid off, moreover—the cloud of economic insecurity that hangs today over so many decent, hardworking Americans—not only increases the formidable stresses of modern life but also heightens racial, ethnic, and generational animosities (black and younger workers generally get laid off before white and older). Insecurity weakens union efforts, company loyalty, and productive teamwork, and even survivors of "reductions in force" do not always see themselves as fortunate. Many, taking on others' jobs in addition to their own, feel overworked; some actually push themselves to the point of exhaustion and burnout in hopes of avoiding a future layoff—not always successfully.

Productivity suffers too among workers worried about being laid off. After the CoreStates Financial Corporation of Philadelphia announced that it would fire 6 percent of its work force, about 890 people, one nervous worker reported: "Everybody's thinking, 'What is my job, what is my future, what am I doing here?' For the last month, people have been talking more than fifty percent of the time. It's water-cooler talk all day long."[7]

Even if all that were not the case, by what right and by what measure of common sense does a supposedly democratic and caring society simply abandon more than 6 percent of its people—most of whom *want* to work—to unemployment, condemn many others to social and economic downscaling, and impose on still others the fear of joblessness? That's bad enough for the present. It's worse for the future because some whose jobs were eliminated in recent years, or soon will be, as well as many who have had no jobs for many years, will never work again. As the population and the would-be labor force increase, while corporations throw people out of work to increase profits, while technology assumes more and more of what once was the work of human hands, jobs just won't be available. Or if a job does come open, it's likely to be low-paying and dead-end.

At the present rate of economic expansion, good only by recession standards, millions of Americans of *all* races, like blacks in the inner city today, are going to be idle, poverty-stricken, likely to become public charges, on welfare, in prison, on the streets. Crime will rise; so will drug reliance. In the ugly British usage, these jobless people, again like today's inner-city blacks, will be "redundant," unneeded waste material. Many already are.

No recent mainstream president or presidential candidate, unless Jesse Jackson is so considered, has promised specifically to seek gains for those at the foot of the economic ladder, certainly not for the black faces at the bottom of the well. Yet all must have been aware of severe economic disparities—for instance, that many whites, including children, as well as blacks, live at or below poverty levels, with more sure to join them. Full employment is a nearly forgotten goal in mainstream politics. Only a new party can revive it.

Full employment, allowing only for some necessary (but lower than 6 percent) level of unemployment, is *not*, moreover, an unattainable goal in the America of the nineties and the coming new century. For one thing, as part of a larger critique of corporate control, a new party dedicated to full employment would preach the revolutionary (in America) doctrine that workers should not be fired or laid off as a first resort when the economy turns sour.

Layoffs should be a *last* resort, not just to preserve the dignity of working Americans but so that they could maintain some level of antirecession purchasing power. This commonsense approach is well understood in Japan, where even in hard times unemployment is much lower than that of Europe and the United States.

That's one example of the relentlessly adversarial position a new party should take toward the corporate economic culture. Another would be an attack on the prevailing mystique that in a competitive world culture, the well-managed "lean and mean" corporation must ruthlessly lay off workers to reduce costs. In the short run, this may make—it has made—U.S. industry more competitive with Hong Kong and Singapore. In a longer view it will create a vast, idle, angry pool of redundant Americans, costly in public services and despoiling the national life through crime and violence, political extremism, possibly revolt. And what good will it do consumer industries or housing construction if economic "necessity" increases the huge percentage of Americans already unemployed or downscaled? Who will be left to buy or build? How many might follow some now-unknown "man on horseback"?

Besides, the "necessity" is too often for the bottom line rather than for economic survival. Corporate profits rose to record levels in 1994: 11 percent, after an even greater rise of 13 percent in 1993. Yet layoffs continued at a pace approaching or exceeding that of the early-nineties recession: half a million jobs in 1994, compared with only 316,047 in 1990 and 555,292 in 1991. Highly profitable companies were still ridding themselves of workers in late 1994 and 1995, well after the economy had recovered.[8]

On the first business day of 1996, AT&T, an icon of American business, announced one of the largest corporate work force reductions in history—forty thousand of its three hundred thousand jobs, more than 13 percent of its workers, in the next three years. That was despite the fact that the gigantic telephone company is profitable and growing.[9]

Corporate America talks competition, of course; in fact, it's now laying off workers and cutting costs in order to increase already swollen profits. Mobil, for example, announced a 9.3 percent work force reduction (forty-seven hundred jobs; forty-seven hundred *people* and their families) in 1995 one week after reporting a profit of $636 million. Mobil stock then jumped to its highest level in fifty-two weeks, a sign that Wall Street, ever alert to the bottom line, approved of the layoffs despite the profits.[10]

A tax system that favors wealth and provides too many escape hatches for corporate income; the long-term trend toward consolidation of economic giants and the further development of monopoly power at the expense of individuals and smaller enterprise; the drastic decline of organized labor—all are issues seldom raised by either major party, thus appropriate to be taken on by one dedicated to economic gains for the have-nots.

More jobs, productive jobs, will have to be created, but that's not an unattainable goal either. Bridges need rebuilding in every state. City streets are a disaster everywhere. The older interstate highways are crumbling. Adequate protection for the environment would require an expansion, not a contraction, of job opportunities. An immense number of structures are inadequately insulated in a nation of profligate energy wastage.

To remedy the latter deficiency—not a high technology task— would have almost immeasurable effects besides putting people to work and training them for useful jobs. It would lower the need for U.S. dependence on oil imports and for burning environmentally destructive coal, help control heating costs and inflationary pressures, diminish pollution and the greenhouse effect.

Great regions of the country are suitable for solar heat, moreover, but now hardly rely on the natural resource of the sun.

Rebuilding the national rail network would be worthwhile now and might well be essential later. Greyhound Bus, once the people's transportation system, is operating in bankruptcy, and the airlines are steadily shrinking in number and routes served. When only two or three airlines monopolize travel, does anyone believe they won't raise fares to levels prohibitive for all but the affluent? And reduce service and eliminate jobs to "cut costs"?

The automobile, clearly the popular favorite of traveling Americans, is costly and polluting and clogs up smog-choked cities. The cost of highways and bridges is extraordinary, and continued reliance on imported oil could make operating an auto even more expensive than it is now. So could a badly needed increase in the federal gasoline tax—in the unlikely event that any national political leader dredges up the nerve and the muscle to put an end to the subsidy American drivers receive in low gasoline taxes.

No major intercity railroad line has been built in the United States since 1924, and Congress is apparently determined to do away with Amtrak, the remnant of a once-vital rail passenger system. Yet numerous intercity corridors suitable for high-speed trains or so-called Maglev development* are available, and a number of states are eager to invest in such projects. Cities smothered by auto traffic cry out for mass transit, despite public and congressional indifference.

One or more major national public works programs (the last was the interstate highway system authorized forty years ago) could take on all these and other chores, filling national needs, employing people, teaching them skills, making useful citizens of many likely now to become welfare recipients, criminals, prostitutes, prison inmates. Good jobs at constructive tasks, paying decent wages, would give such people what President Clinton in his much-applauded speech at Memphis in November 1993 called "the structure, the values, the discipline, and the reward that work gives." They need little else so much.

Even the hardest-nosed conservatives will hardly dispute this proposition; work, after all, is at the center of their proclaimed values. The private sector, moreover, with its expertise and resources, necessarily would be involved. So these projects, with their subsidiary effects, as did the building of the interstate highway system in the fifties, would bring about business expansion and the training and employment of even more people. That's another conservative goal, or ought to be.

Conservatives also decry the federal deficit, however, and a

---

*Maglev trains travel at high speeds on a cushion of air, needing roadbeds but not tracks. Some authorities think such trains could be feasible in the United States in the relatively near future.

public works program on the necessary scale unquestionably would increase the deficit in the short run. But such projects, worthwhile in themselves, also would be an investment in the long run, leading to increased economic activity, expanded taxpayer rolls, lessened welfare expenditures, decreased costs of crime and punishment, even lower tax rates. Well-run businesses seldom hesitate to make investments that are costly now but justifiable later. So here's another place where conservatives are right when they say that the government should be run more like a business—but wrong if they argue that only cutting costs is businesslike.

The precipitate loss of decent jobs and decent wages was the most important factor in the explosive growth of the underclass in the 1970s and its continuing, blighting presence.* To make income-earning jobs generally available to what are now inner-city residents, therefore, and to equip them to get and keep such jobs are important corollaries to the overall goal of full employment. It might even prove an effective anticrime program.

No one can pretend, however, that putting jobs into the inner city for its residents to fill would be an easy task. Quite the opposite. The frequently touted panacea of "job training" certainly is not enough. Even if in the era of technology adequate training programs for ill-educated persons could be devised, and if they could be made attractive to undisciplined ghetto youth, they would do little good if they only spewed jobless people back to the mean streets whence they came. Jobs, good jobs, have to be available at the end of the training pipeline.

If no such jobs await, the trainees are likely to believe that only a placebo has been offered in the few weeks of training— not a real remedy for a real malady. All too often, unfortunately, that has been the truth of well-intended job-training programs.

Even affluent, entrepreneurial blacks with the best will in the world can bring few jobs to the ghetto. The almost entirely white lords of the U.S. economy might—if they would. But bottom-line

*As will be discussed in Chapter Nine.

considerations make it unlikely that even the most public-spirited corporations actually will put major operations into the ghetto. More willing and skilled workers, at the same or lower wages, in better social and working conditions, can be found almost anywhere outside the big-city ghetto—foreign countries included. Nor would middle management and skilled technologists be likely to want to go to work every day in the dismal and dangerous South Bronx or any other inner-city neighborhood.

Substantial incentives might—or might not—lure owners and managers of job-providing enterprises to set up shop in the ghetto, finding and training their workers from among those available nearby. But such incentives are not in the political cards. President Clinton has proposed nothing of the sort. In a time of budget constraint and animosity toward racial integration, neither Congress nor any state, much less the taxpayer, seems willing to take such costly, problematical steps.

The idea of "ghetto renewal" may be illusory in any case. One who thinks so is Nicholas Lemann, the chronicler[11] of the great post–World War II black migration out of southern cotton fields and into American cities:

> Of all the dramatic solutions to the problems of the ghettos, probably the most common and persistent for the past quarter century has been the idea that they can be "developed" into thriving ethnic enclaves. . . . Such proposals have a powerful emotional attractiveness. They envelop the ghettos in the romanticized aura that Americans attach to small-town life.

Lemann believes, however, that "the clear lesson of experience" is that this kind of "ghetto development hasn't worked." Nor does he think it *can* work: "[T]he reality is that our ghettos bear the accumulated weight of all the bad in our country's racial history, and they are now among the worst places to live in the world."

Why should blacks or anyone be expected to work or live in such areas? Lemann asks, pointing out that European immigrants of a century ago "had no intention of making the ghetto their permanent residence."[12]

In a panel discussion at Harvard's Kennedy School of Government, Margaret Weir of the Brookings Institution advocated instead a federal effort to "promote the mobility of the urban poor," in much the same way that government policies have helped whites to move out of cities into suburbs. Such mobility would increase what she called "access to prosperity" for the underclass and "help poor people as well as poor places."[13]

That approach also presents numerous difficulties. White suburbanites as well as working-class whites and middle-class blacks in better urban neighborhoods will not welcome inner-city blacks. They fear the lawlessness some might bring along, and they would resent feared newcomers being imposed on often close-knit areas by government policy.

Ghetto "dispersal," moreover, is not always a popular idea even among blacks concerned about the inner city. Dispersal smacks too much of "forced removal" or, more cynically, "Negro removal." African-Americans learned to be wary of such plans from the old "slum clearance" programs that made urban land available for many a luxurious apartment building only whites could afford. And dispersal would make little allowance for the solid working-class families that somehow have remained in the inner city.

Some black elected officials would object, even if selfishly, to diminution of their inner-city political bases. Other African-Americans, accustomed to doubting white motives, might believe that was the real objective: to diminish black voting strength in the cities. In some cases it might be.

If "ghetto renewal" and "ghetto dispersal" are unpromising approaches to redeeming the inner city, what's left? The range of approaches to the problems of the underclass are certainly limited. But that's not a reason for giving up, for writing off generations of African-Americans who, as things now appear, will be forever lost to productive citizenship and the good American life.

Part of the answer is that nationwide public works program—rebuilding streets, highways, bridges, railways—and the business and industrial expansion it would spark. Such a renewal of the national infrastructure would symbolize, perhaps even inspire a larger national renewal.

Another vital part of the answer is improved public education, in general and in the inner city. Too many of today's school-children are being shortchanged by public and taxpayer apathy; by crime- and fear-ridden schools in the inner city that teach little more than survival; by schools elsewhere that focus on driver training and sports; by shortsighted, selfish, sometimes corrupt unions; by legislative indifference and political hostility to "spending" and taxes; by an imbalance of resources favoring affluent over poor school districts.

Privatization of some public schools, competition between these and remaining public schools, vouchers to enable parents to choose more promising schools for their children—such conservative proposals deserve comprehensive testing and adoption where proved effective. They do *not* justify a precipitate turn from the public education that has been vital to the nation's development.

However it's done, the rejuvenation of public education is vital to the redemption of the ghetto. And for this purpose too, economic gains for the poor are all-important, tending, as they would, to improve the social and physical environment of families, upgrade student behavior and performance, and—not least—yield more political "clout" to those who now have little.

Perhaps more important than any specific proposal would be the fact of a new party—the political pressure it would bring, win or lose, on the mainstream parties. Such a party would make it impossible for the Democrats to court middle-class white votes while depending on the votes of poor blacks. Republicans could no longer slight the interests of more than forty million Americans living in poverty.

A new party's activities and votes would focus public attention on the needs of the poor and disadvantaged, including the African-Americans for so long victimized by American society, and on the attitudes of those who no longer believe in the promise of democracy. These, rather than the supposed miseries of the relatively well-off white middle class, are the gravest threats to the national future. These are the proper objects of an enlightened politics.

The major parties, however, are not going to recognize that, the Republicans because their interest is in the middle class and white communities, the Democrats because they are trying to compete with the Republicans. Both parties' political pitch is to the middle class, not to an underclass that hangs like a dark cloud over the future of American cities and American life.

"We all know [the underclass] is the principal problem in American domestic life," Nicholas Lemann has written, "a problem that poisons not just race relations but also our attitudes toward education, law enforcement, and city life itself."[14]

"We all" may *know* that; unfortunately we all—most particularly the Democratic and Republican parties—neither admit it nor want to do anything effective about it. Consequently those parties will not think, much less do anything useful, about the problems of the underclass or the unemployed or the nonvoters.

Only a new party, formed for that purpose, made up principally of those to be redeemed, will take up the cause of these virtually forgotten Americans. Only a new party will devote its best minds and its best efforts to their cause. And only a new party's political determination and dedicated votes can see to it that the rest of us pay attention.

6 How Level the Field?

Your race suffer very greatly, many of them,
from living among us.

Abraham Lincoln
(to a black delegation)

After legal segregation had been ended in the South, as John
Hope Franklin recalls, whites reacted "as if there were no
black culture and no black history." Everything was expected to
change for blacks, but whites still would be, as they always had
been, the dominant race.

Decades later, as emeritus professor of history at Duke University
and one of the sanest American voices on race relations,
Franklin still could mock what he recalled as the typical white
attitude of the sixties: "Now that you've got civil rights and the
vote, what else can you possibly want? Surely you don't want to
be chief executive at the bank? Surely you can't want to join
our clubs?"

In the forties Franklin taught at North Carolina College in Durham,
one of the all-black institutions that state maintained in its
supposedly "separate but equal" higher education system. Franklin
did his historical research, however, at the nearby Duke Uni-

versity library; the Duke faculty made him welcome in the stacks "but of course never invited me to their offices or anything like that."

A distinguished Duke professor, a native of Mississippi, accosted him one day and said, "Franklin, I hear you're against segregation."

Franklin admitted it. Whereupon the white professor, genuinely bewildered, asked: "How can you possibly be? That means you're against your own interests. Without segregation, all the blacks would come to Duke and you'd be out of a job at NCC."

The white professor could not conceive that anything was "salvageable" in black culture. He assumed instead that if segregation ended, all blacks would rush to join established white society (transferring symbolically from inferior NCC to superior Duke).

The white professor assumed also that *he* had nothing to fear from black academics, that whites would continue to dominate white institutions, with or without segregation. John Hope Franklin, although the gentlest of men, was not one to acquiesce in this easy assumption. If segregation were ended, he replied, and blacks did indeed transfer from NCC to Duke, then he certainly would come after the white professor's job.[1]

A half century later he had the equivalent. Most blacks had not been so successful.

Not until the fifties and sixties, through court decisions and legislation, did the "land of the free" abolish legally established segregation in the South, and that Duke professor's expectations suggest the contempt in which most African-Americans were held nearly a century after emancipation.

Even in 1956, two years after school segregation had been ruled unconstitutional, the historian Kenneth Stampp encountered—"to my surprise," he recalled years later—difficulty with his seminal book about American slavery, *The Peculiar Institution*. The executive editor of a major publishing house asked him: "Would a book about slavery deal with a subject that was little more than 'a large footnote to American history'?"[2]

The historian did not need to specify that the executive editor of a major publishing house in 1956 was white, as indeed he or she probably would be today. But in the nineties, owing to the work of Stampp and others, fewer whites might consider black enslavement—the defining event in the heritage of millions of their fellow citizens, something like the nation's "original sin"— a mere footnote to American history.

More than halfway through the twentieth century, southern blacks still endured segregation and all African-Americans lived with a sort of genetic memory of hundreds of years in which some of their parents and many of their ancestors had been chattel slaves. Enslavement had been followed by another century in which de jure segregation was a southern manifestation of a de facto national attitude. Only the most remarkable African-American could have escaped psychological damage from knowledge of the captive status into which the race had been cast, for so long, by a white society dominant since James-town and Plymouth.

In its infamous *Dred Scott* decision the Supreme Court held in the mid-nineteenth century that blacks had no rights that white people were bound to respect. By the end of the century the High Court had upheld legal segregation. Even the Great Emancipator, believing it unlikely that the two races could live in harmony, had thought it best that blacks should be sent to Africa or to Central America.

"Your race suffer very greatly, many of them, by living among us" (as was certainly true), he told a black delegation to the White House, "while ours suffer from your presence" (which brought on a great war).*

Even after emancipation, southern whites, with the conniv-ance of northern politicians, contrived the sharecrop system, by which millions of blacks and not a few poor whites were kept in virtual bondage. For nearly a century the Supreme Court as

---

*August 14, 1862. Neither Lincoln nor anyone else suggested that whites should go back to Europe and leave the New World to blacks.

well as white Americans sanctioned "separate but equal" (in practice, inferior) facilities in the South for blacks: schools, drinking fountains, railroad cars, eating places, toilets, seats in theaters and at baseball games.

For blacks in the South in the days of segregation, moreover, fear was a constant: fear of lynching, fear of loss of livelihood, fear of whites. Randall Kennedy of the Harvard Law School faculty still remembers an incident from his childhood when white policemen stopped his family's auto for no other reason than to demand to know what they were doing in the South.[3]

David L. Evans, now and for many years an admissions officer at Harvard, once read a book about the Scottsboro Boys. The book caused him constant worry that their fate might befall him, as in Helena, Arkansas, in 1952, to an African-American youth, it well might have. Later, as a NASA engineer at Huntsville, Alabama, near Scottsboro, Evans read an article about an old judge who had presided in one of the Scottsboro trials. As Evans remembers the article, the old judge* said something to the effect: "Sure, I knew they were innocent. But I had to live there."[4]

Evans, though a mild-mannered man, wanted to go to nearby Scottsboro "and throw a brick through his window."

In my North Carolina hometown in the thirties and forties, black yard help would be handed a plate of food out the back door when "dinnertime" arrived. It was unthinkable that a black worker might be invited to eat at the kitchen table. Later the plate would be thoroughly scalded, lest something "catching" might linger on it. Nor was this precaution concealed from the yard help.

To prove that whites have not really treated blacks too badly, even in the South, some like to cite a contradictory history of intimate or at least friendly black-white personal associations, not usually including, of course, the miscegenation of the southern white male ruling class with the black women they forced into sexual submission during and after enslavement. These

---

*Evans did not recall the judge's name, but he was probably A. E. Hawkins of Scottsboro, who sat in the first trial. James E. Horton, Jr., of Decatur, Alabama, presided over a subsequent trial.

arguments emphasize instead the easy relations of white employers and black house servants, usually presented as not unlike Mammy in *Gone With the Wind*.

Contemplating black-white relationships, the African-American psychologist Dr. Kenneth Clark observed:

> [R]acial problems have not been problems of racial contact.... It is not the sitting next to a white, *but the fact that this implies equal status*. Historically, the most intimate relationships have been approved ... so long as [the] status of white superiority versus Negro inferiority has been clear. Trouble comes only when Negroes ... seek a status equal to that of whites.[5]

At the Winston-Salem, North Carolina, *Journal*, where I worked in the fifties, a lone black reporter covered the city's "colored news"; a single page in the Sunday edition was deemed sufficient for his entire week's report: births, deaths, weddings, graduations, everything. The black reporter was required by the management to use a toilet set aside for the black janitors while white reporters were afforded larger, better facilities—not because the black reporter was less clean or fastidious than they but because his use of the white reporters' washroom would have implied an equal status still unacknowledged in the South long after *Brown* v. *Board,* the Supreme Court decision outlawing segregation in public schools. To my lasting shame, I did not protest this arrangement.

On the other hand, one of the other white reporters, a sophisticated man from a nonsouthern state, told me that of course he welcomed the end of legal segregation—but he did not want to swim in the same municipal pool with blacks. He was not worried about equality but about blacks' supposed lack of hygiene (then widely assumed by whites).

During much of American history, African-Americans were not allowed to seek or hold public office anywhere. In the South and in parts of all regions they were not even allowed the vote or were hampered in its exercise. Lyndon Johnson, as he proposed what became the Voting Rights Act of 1965, described a black political plight that he knew at first hand, in his native Texas:

> The Negro citizen may go to register, only to be told that the day is wrong or the hour is late or the official in charge is absent. . . . [I]f he manages to present himself to the registrar, he may be disqualified because he did not spell out his middle name or because he abbreviated a word. . . . [I]f he manages to fill out an application, he is given a test. The registrar is the sole judge of whether he passes. . . . He may be asked to recite the entire Constitution. . . . And even a college degree cannot be used to prove that he can read and write.

LBJ, ever aware of southern power in the Congress of that day—white segregationist power—was too politic to speak of blacks denied jobs for trying to vote or of Klan-style physical intimidation, including lynching, that often had prevented black suffrage.

Unfortunately, when southern segregation was abolished in the sixties, few white persons either knew or credited the crippling disabilities that slavery and second-class status had wrought in their victims or the deep-seated prejudices that had been created in white attitudes. Whites could and did congratulate themselves on the apparent triumph of equality in America.

Never mind that the "triumph" had been hundreds of years in the making and was stoutly resisted to the end, not just by Klansmen and "rednecks" but often in the most respectable circles. The prevalent impression in 1964 and 1965 was that the nation actually had reached the lofty ideals expressed in the Declaration of Independence and the Constitution, the words of Abraham Lincoln, and boilerplate speeches by generations of insincere or ignorant politicians.

In fact, the white society that controlled the nation had done only what it had *had* to do—reluctantly at that. Legislation and court rulings had barely outpaced the largely nonviolent race rebellion of the civil rights movement. If the end of segregation was proper in 1964, moreover, America had done only what should have been done decades earlier.

Senator Everett McKinley Dirksen, the mellifluent Illinois Republican whose influence as Senate minority leader was vital to passage of the Civil Rights Act of 1964, spoke in debate of the power of "an idea whose time has come." Dirksen's vote and leadership in a Senate nominally controlled by Democrats and southerners were bold, but his oratory was a century overdue. The idea, if not the fact, of equality for blacks went back at least to the Emancipation Proclamation by another Illinois Republican, in 1862.

Abolishing legal segregation in the South, which was what the nation actually did in the 1960s, was *all* that most Americans believed needed to be done. The years of open civil rights agitation from the mid-fifties to the mid-sixties and the resulting legislation and court decisions had been directed *against segregation in the South*. Inequality in the nation had not really been at issue.

The Freedom Riders had gone South, not North or West. Martin Luther King had met his most significant failure when he tried to carry the civil rights movement into Chicago. Americans had been properly shocked when they read in their newspapers about—particularly when they saw on the screens that flickered in an ever-rising number of living rooms—Police Commissioner Bull Connor's dogs and water cannon and cattle prods routing black demonstrators (including children) in Birmingham.

Good citizens were not aroused by stories of segregated housing or lily-white construction unions in northern cities because there were few such stories; anyway, that kind of thing was not written into local laws. Editorial anger had focused on southern segregation, not on northern school systems that were to remain largely all-white for decades to come.

Segregation in the South had openly contradicted American ideals, offended many Americans' self-perception, embarrassed the nation abroad, and was easy for nonsoutherners—and even many southern whites—to condemn. Besides, to residents of Michigan and Wisconsin and Vermont, the South seemed almost another country. Whites could deplore abuses in the faraway

South while smugly assuming that *their* home states or cities did not tolerate such repression and inequality, certainly not by law.

Thus honorable and concerned whites from Cleveland and Chicago and New York flocked to Selma, Alabama, in the sixties without realizing or admitting that flourishing discrimination needed to be fought in their own communities. And going South to march against George Wallace and the Klan was the more gratifying to the white conscience because it definitely could be dangerous; it could be lethal, as it was in Mississippi in 1964.

Northern whites who personally supported black demonstrators in the South did a decent and courageous thing. But a higher perception would have been required for marching *at home* against the practical fact of discrimination where it was neither legally decreed nor generally admitted—but omnipresent nevertheless.

Apartheid in the South, as it existed before the mid-sixties, was in fact only the most egregious offense against the nation's stated ideals; hence southern segregation was the obvious target for blacks and liberals alike. But to some whites forty-odd years ago—and no doubt to some still today—it was the *only* target, the *only* offense that needed to be eliminated.

The Kerner Commission estimated in 1968 that all Americans then living below the poverty line could be brought up to that level (eliminating *poverty* but not the poor and not the difference between rich and poor) by targeted federal expenditures of eleven billion dollars. That probably reflected too little knowledge of poverty, but it was not an impossible economic goal: Eleven billion dollars were not a large share of gross national product in the sixties and were well within the nation's economic capacity.

In fact, government action—"spending" was not then so widely despised as it is now—actually got results. Johnson's "war on poverty," though derided today, by 1969 had reduced the poverty population "by about one third, from 36 million in 1964 to only slightly over 24 million. . . . The percentage of the population living below the poverty line had fallen from 19 percent to 12.1 percent."[6]

Spending for the poor improved their circumstances then. Despite critics' protests, it still does.

> Federal, state and local governments spent about $300 billion on programs for the poor in 1993, the last year for which we have complete accounts. The six biggest programs were Medicaid ($132 billion), food stamps ($26 billion), Supplemental Security Income, ($26 billion), Aid to Families with Dependent Children ($25 billion), and low-income housing subsidies ($20 billion), and Head Start and other compensatory education ($10 billion). Medicaid, food stamps, housing subsidies, and S.S.I. clearly did what they were meant to do. A.F.D.C. and compensatory education programs have had mixed records, but neither is a clear failure.[7]

African-Americans were significantly affected by the war on poverty; unfortunately it did not last. The late-sixties riots in the cities further inflamed backlash among whites generally, George Wallace was effectively lampooning the "pointyheads" in Washington "who don't know how to park their bicycles," and the election of Richard Nixon as president in November 1968 signaled an end to most of the war on poverty.

By 1976 the poverty population was back up to twenty-five million, approximately the level of 1964, and by 1983, midway in President Reagan's first term, thirty-three million Americans were living in poverty. A major reason for this relapse was the shortsighted view of Americans that an end to legal segregation in the South meant an end to the disadvantages of African-Americans generally, so that they needed no more help.

Black progress, it was generally recognized, would take some years. But in time, surely, African-Americans would become comfortable, prosperous, middle-class citizens, not disturbing, of course, the inferiority-superiority pattern of black-white relations cited by Kenneth Clark. Life then could go on as before, with no great disturbance for the generous whites who had given blacks such a great opportunity.

That was the nub of it. White America had done what it had had to do *and neither wanted nor saw the need to do more*. It was up to African-Americans to find their improved place and keep to it, fitting themselves with as little disruption as possible into the good society created by white energy and ingenuity and persistence. Thus the end of legal segregation brought a boastful phrase into currency: *The playing field has been leveled.*

Few added a qualifying "after three and a half centuries of discrimination." But a predictable corollary did go with this self-congratulation. If both races were playing on a level field, could not, should not each individual, black or white, run the races—to complete the string of clichés—of economic and social life for him or herself, expecting and deserving no help from anyone?

This "color-blind" attitude (after centuries of blatant color consciousness) overlooked the fact that those centuries of discrimination had significantly diminished the economic competition encountered by whites. Loud proclamations of white self-sufficiency ignored a more subtle truth: The incalculable value of being white in America rested to a large extent on the calculable disadvantage of being black.

The relegation of blacks to subordinate status had created two vastly different classes (not just colors) of Americans: white and black, categories far more definitive and irrevocable than all other divisions. Most immigrants had at least the one qualification, white skin, absolutely required for ultimate acceptance in the dominant group. Haitians, Jamaicans, and Hispanic blacks need not apply. Neither could native-born blacks.

The disadvantages suffered by many white immigrants—the Irish, for perhaps the most prominent example—were real but outweighed by a single unearned advantage: With all other whites, they could look down the well at the black faces on the bottom. So the successive waves of immigrants and the poor native-born whites who "made good" in American society *did* receive important help: the racially discriminatory practices legal in the South and common everywhere in America that gave whites advantages—preferences, in fact—over millions of native blacks who were not allowed to compete.

*　　*　　*

Persons bought, held, and exploited in slavery could hardly be regarded as equals, and in early America it quickly became part of slaveowners' and slavery defenders' justifications that an enslaved race was less developed and less capable of development than their own. The Confederacy fought the bloodiest, most destructive war in American history to defend that belief.

Early in this century a white Georgian named Ulrich B. Phillips published *American Negro Slavery*, the first comprehensive study of the subject. Phillips concluded that Africans "by racial inequality" had submitted to bondage more easily than white Europeans would have. This arbitrary judgment, appearing in a book featuring much factual research on other matters, was widely accepted by whites.

Blacks, after all, are the only sizable group in American history to have been chattel slaves. The resulting heritage is a heavy burden for contemporary African-Americans, despite studies subsequent to Phillips's detailing the fortitude and dignity with which most of their ancestors endured their ordeal. The debilities imposed by centuries of slavery and more than a century of segregation, discrimination, and degradation have left many African-Americans unable to compete with whites, economically or socially.

Whites tend to see and sneer at the inability without understanding the history. As Andrew Hacker has suggested, they seem to nurse an inchoate suspicion about people who once were enslaved: "Might there be something about the black race that suited them for slavery?"[8]

This suspicion has been lent apparently impressive support— for instance, by William Shockley and Arthur Jensen, both noted academics. Shockley's work locates blacks lower on the evolutionary scale than Europeans; Jensen's studies have led him to assert that black children cannot profit from compensatory education because they are genetically inferior, not merely ill taught. Few scientists of stature concur with either man, but many unscientific Americans seem willing to believe that blacks aren't capable of equality with whites.

As late as 1994 Charles Murray and the late Richard J. Herrnstein published *The Bell Curve*, with its supposedly scientific conclusion that intelligence, as measured by IQ tests, is inherited and cannot be enhanced after childhood. If that were so, remedial efforts or environmental influences could not have much effect. Most African-Americans record lower IQ scores than whites, so *The Bell Curve* would condemn them genetically to a lower place on the economic and social scale than whites can achieve.

The Bell Curve received almost universal rejection in the black community and much condemnation as "pseudoscience" from authorities other than the authors'. They had not taken account of some studies contradicting their findings—a 1961 survey of the out-of-wedlock children of black and white U.S. soldiers and German mothers, for instance. That study allowed for differences in pre- and postnatal care and found a small IQ difference that actually favored the black children.

Nevertheless, many white Americans believed *The Bell Curve* had confirmed their suspicion—put bluntly, that blacks are intellectually and genetically inferior.

In 1989 an official Task Force on Minorities, Equity and Excellence recommended further multicultural reform of New York State's public school curriculum, which already had been changed, in 1987, to include more study of non-European cultures. A commentator on this bristling report evoked much derision when he advocated reference to "enslaved persons" rather than to "slaves."

A difference without a distinction! "Political correctness" carried to an extreme! cried many whites, already offended by the report itself. But the real distinction between forcibly "enslaved persons" and perhaps voluntarily submissive "slaves" cannot be easily dismissed, and the outcry seemed to emphasize Hacker's hard speculation that whites tend to lump "blacks" and "slaves" into one contemptible category.

"Enslaved persons" conveys the opposite idea: that if someone has been "enslaved," someone else forced the chains upon the victim. And someone did in the case of enslaved persons in the American South; those euphemistically termed "masters" in most history texts were actually "enslavers," including George Washington, Thomas Jefferson, James Madison, and any number of Confederate war heroes.

During the Civil War Abraham Lincoln took mocking note of the hesitant attempts of "our erring brothers" to enlist their black slaves as Confederate soldiers: "I have in my lifetime heard many arguments why the Negroes ought to be slaves; but if they fight for those who would keep them in slavery it will be a better argument than any I have yet heard."[9]

In fact, the Confederates risked putting only one out of four male slaves in uniform, and that only when the southern rebellion was near its end and in desperate need of manpower.

As detailed in earlier chapters, white backlash began in the sixties almost as soon as the civil rights movement appeared to have triumphed. Whites were disappointed and many were angered that the end of legal segregation in the South had increased pressures for African-American social and economic equality everywhere, thus for further disruptions of settled white life.

Blacks too were disappointed in the course of events after the long-desired end of legal segregation. Overoptimistically, they had expected to be more widely accepted into American society and to move up more rapidly in the economic world.[10] The legal and legislative successes of the civil rights movement and the advents of the politically friendly Democratic Presidents Kennedy and Johnson produced a sense among blacks that an era had ended and another was beginning. That was true, but not quite as they thought.

"In the enthusiasm of the period," Dr. Kenneth Clark recalled many years later, "it was not clear to many of us that racism was not limited to its flagrant forms found in the southern states, where the glaring abuses could be remedied by litigation. We soon found that there were deeper, more profound forms of racial injustice to be found in northern states."[11]

Psychiatrist Dr. Alvin Poussaint also recalls rather sadly that the civil rights movement and the black community generally had "underestimated . . . the entrenchment in the culture of certain beliefs"—white prejudice.

As the sixties passed, moreover, Dr. Poussaint became convinced that most whites were not ready for true integration. White flight from newly desegregated public schools and the proliferation in the South of "Christian" all-white academies supported his belief. So did continuing housing and neighborhood segregation, job disparities, and second-class status for most African-Americans.

In the decades after southern apartheid was abolished, few African-Americans could fail to notice that school desegregation was marked more prominently by white mobs in Little Rock and Boston than by black faces in formerly all-white classrooms; that not much had changed economically or socially for the masses of black people outside the South; that despite federal, state, and sometimes even local action to end discrimination in housing, bank and automobile loans, football coaching ranks, the jury box, corporate promotions, etc., white America was finding ingenious or merely brazen ways to circumvent these efforts.

That "the more things change, the more they are the same" was evident in many ways:

John Hope Franklin has pointed out that although today's college campuses are "integrated," before the sixties most were all-white and had been closed to blacks for centuries. But then the "gate [was] unlocked and we expect[ed] blacks to wander in there and find their way around and become a part of the community."[12]

A quarter century after Congress had passed major civil rights legislation, Henry Louis Gates moved from one prestigious university, Duke, to head the black studies program at another, Harvard. He took up residence in Lexington, Massachusetts, a predominantly white suburb of Boston. Right away Gates visited the Lexington police station, made himself known there as "Dr. Gates" of Harvard, and explained that he was living in Lexington and therefore might often be seen driving on its streets. He did not want to be pulled over in his car, perhaps arrested, for being seen where he knew white policemen were likely to think no black person should be.[13]

For blacks and other minorities in 1957, median family income—a powerful indicator—had been about $10,000 compared with $18,250 for whites.* Ten years later, with southern segregation dismantled by courts and Congress, three civil rights bills passed, the Voting Rights Act in place, and Lyndon Johnson's war on poverty under way (also, unfortunately, his war in Vietnam), median family income for blacks alone had risen to about $14,500 while that of whites had reached $25,000. The differential in favor of whites—$8,250 in 1957—actually had *increased* to $10,500 in 1967.[14]

During the sixties and seventies, even after affirmative action efforts in higher education, the black share of places on the faculties of predominantly white universities grew only from near zero to about 2 percent.[15] This was a welcome gain, of course, especially to those in the 2 percent, most of whom were classic examples of the Jackie Robinson syndrome.

The first black player in the major baseball leagues, Robinson was an athletic superstar, formerly a standout football player at UCLA. Had he been merely an average infielder, he would never have been forced upon a lily-white and resistant system by the Brooklyn Dodgers, though then and now there were any number of "merely average" (by major-league standards) white players. For years after Robinson and the Dodgers broke the color line, few, if any, "merely average" black players could make such a breakthrough.

Nearly fifty years later, in the nineties, the major leagues no longer require African-Americans to be superstars. They too can be "merely average" on one of the few playing fields in American life that even comes close to being level.

---

*Round numbers based on Census Bureau findings.

7 Feeding the Backlash

The notion that affirmative action should be completely stripped away is ridiculous. Anyone who would suggest that racism is a thing of the past is wrong.

Colin Powell
(quoted by
the New York Daily News)

Afte 1965 a new kind of Negro began to appear, younger and more assertive than their elders, preferring to call themselves blacks—until later, when for some "African-American" became the preferred self-description.

These blacks were willing to assert the values—and the *value*—of their own culture and seemed less interested in being like, or liked by, white persons than in being free and equal American citizens. Boldly they attacked the many discriminatory white practices and institutions still thriving: biased admissions policies at prestigious universities, unrepresentative political bodies, lily-white corporations and unions, exclusionary professional associations.

Alvin Poussaint, bred in an older tradition, did not disapprove of the new blacks but wondered whether their independence would be as productive politically as a more moderate approach.

But one day, rather to his surprise, he found himself asserting his own black pride, his own professional needs, as an organizer of the Black Psychiatrists of America.[1]

The new black was a predictable figure. Given the history of Negroes in America, younger blacks naturally were eager to be free of conditions that had limited their forebears' lives. So they banded together (with an American faith in organization) in the various forms of the black power movement.

It was also natural that given the same history, whites resented and feared black power rhetoric. Where was these people's gratitude? Hadn't generous whites given them enough when segregation was banned? When the vote was guaranteed?

In fact, the black power movement was a direct, not merely implicit, challenge to what Kenneth Clark cited as the prerequisite of the old stable black-white relationship: tacitly acknowledged white superiority, tacitly accepted black inferiority. Few whites had imagined *that* bedrock could crumble, even after desegregation in faraway Dixieland.

Mainstream black leaders like Martin Luther King had been threatening enough to established order, accepted values. But King at least had preached Gandhian nonviolence, not black power. An unspoken fear of black rape and revolt was as much a part of the white heritage as slavery was of African-Americans' collective psyche. Some whites shuddered therefore to imagine in black power rhetoric ("Violence is as American as cherry pie," proclaimed H. Rap Brown) revolutionary echoes of Nat Turner and John Brown.

Such words, such attitudes, seemed "a slap in the face" rather than the grateful response to white America's concessions that most whites thought reasonable. Just as President Kennedy and his brother Robert had tried to hold back the Freedom Riders' ventures into the South, hoping to avoid angering southern whites, moderate leaders urged organizations like the Black Panthers and SNCC* not to "rock the boat" or irritate the white majority.

Black power talk, solemn analysis in the press asserted, was "hurting the black cause." In fact, it was hurting the feelings and raising the fears of whites, who had wanted integration, if at all, on *their* terms, not on those of the black militants. And it was demanding further action that few whites wanted to take or had believed they ever would have to.

Black youths, however, as they shook off the effects of historic white domination, did not see why they should be silent about their legitimate desire for full citizenship or the need for anti-discrimination action outside the South. Their militance stiffened in the face of white resentment; black "demands," often "non-negotiable," began to be heard. Black rhetoric rose in stridency, and not a few whites considered it insolence.

"Outlandish" demands (such as "reparations" for slavery—how much? paid to whom?) and militant blacks' "brazen" speeches suggested to white America that they had been "given too much," so had come to expect even more and to demand it in the rudest terms. Here again was a profound white misunderstanding.

African-Americans had suffered such oppression for so long that it was remarkable they had not risen in violent wrath, like the Mau Maus of Kenya. "Giving" them civil rights and the vote—to which, in fact, they always should have been as entitled as any American—was *not* a generous white concession. It was a long-delayed, fiercely resisted, politically *forced* recognition of blacks' stolen birthright, a tacit acknowledgment that a great wrong had been done.

If it was not a wrong, why had it needed to be corrected? And if it *was* a wrong, why should blacks be grateful or tender toward the feelings of those whose race had perpetrated it? And

*The Student Nonviolent Coordinating Committee, despite its name, became one of the most militant black organizations after Stokely Carmichael took over its leadership.

why should not those escaping oppression, like prisoners escaping confinement, feel the need to stretch their muscles?

It's perhaps arguable that black humility might have been tactically more acceptable than black pride. But does not that argument—that blacks should have pulled the forelock rather than shake the fist—presuppose black inequality and white superiority? Doesn't it suggest that whites can be aggressive, and certainly are, but blacks should be humble?

African-Americans, however, *had* been humble, and for centuries. In the fifties, moreover, white leaders had offered little in return except the advice to "be patient" still longer. Martin Luther King and his brethren had chosen action instead and got results. So it's not surprising that African-Americans in the years after desegregation had little confidence in humility's capacity to move white America, and less desire to try it.

White Americans, however, were aghast to find that blacks (like John Hope Franklin) not only wanted to be fully equal citizens—in the entire nation, not just the South—but would act on the desire. Not for the last time in a world of grievances was it seen that partial redress is rarely enough; once the process of making amends is begun, it's hard to stop short of full redemption.

In the late sixties black leaders in Charlotte, North Carolina, went into federal court to seek a desegregated school system in that city, as promised a decade earlier in *Brown* v. *Board*. Their lead counsel was Julius Chambers, later a high official of the NAACP Legal Defense Fund, still later the chancellor of North Carolina College, his formerly all-black alma mater.

As Chambers piled up the evidence, the white federal judge hearing the case was dismayed. Over the years, Robert McMillan learned, Mecklenburg County school boards (controlled by white men he knew and respected) had systematically located Charlotte's school buildings not where population growth might have indicated but in response to the city's established patterns of residential segregation by race. A rigidly segregated dual school system had resulted and been maintained in a growing, changing, and supposedly "progressive" city.

In his *Mecklenburg* decision, the fair-minded and courageous Judge McMillan ordered white and black children to be transported by bus (many for long distances) to newly desegregated schools. That was the only logical means of desegregating a school system segregated by school building placement. On paper, moreover, busing did not seem a particularly revolutionary approach; rural pupils all over the country had been transported for decades to town schools in the yellow buses so familiar that Norman Rockwell had painted one for a *Saturday Evening Post* cover.

In the South, however, many a rural *white* youth had been bused right past the schoolhouse nearest his or her home—a *segregated* school, for black children only.*

The decision might have been logical, but that did not stop Charlotte from erupting in anger. Chambers's law offices were firebombed; Judge McMillan found that white men at his country club would no longer play golf with him. In Charlotte and elsewhere, as court-ordered school desegregation continued, nothing proved more inflammatory than busing.†

Nonetheless the *Mecklenburg* decision became law, upheld by the Supreme Court, and busing frequently was ordered in other cities. White parents bitterly protested. Some black parents too

---

*Judge McMillan himself had lived as a child in a rural area of Robeson County, North Carolina, and had been bused to school in Fairmont, North Carolina. Later he attended law school at the University of North Carolina; still later he was appointed to the federal bench by President Johnson.
†Busing and desegregation ultimately helped Charlotte become one of the South's most prosperous cities. Long after the *Mecklenburg* decision Judge McMillan and Julius Chambers were honored at a community banquet at which I was pleased to be the principal speaker. And when President Reagan, cavalier with facts as usual, denounced busing in Charlotte in 1984, the local *Observer* denounced *him* for not knowing what he was talking about.

resisted having their children bused to distant, perhaps hostile areas. And the "race mixing" that resulted seemed to many whites to go beyond desegregation of schools or even "racial balance" to what they had never approved: "forced integration." White mobs throwing rocks at busloads of black children were only the most extreme of the responses.

The inherent problems of school desegregation were intensified. Many black teachers, often not as educationally qualified as white teachers, at least by bureaucratic measure, lost their jobs as busing brought consolidation of black and white schools. White teachers, unaccustomed to black pupils who had not the home, economic, social, and educational advantages of whites, quickly became discouraged, even embittered by their new, often unruly classes and the poor educational performances of many of their new pupils. White parents, reacting sometimes racially but possibly as often from the wish to give their children educational advantages, found new interest in "Christian" all-white private schools that multiplied in the South. More legitimate private schools flourished as well, and white flight became one of the larger difficulties of public schools everywhere.

The problems of black pupils in formerly white schools— lower reading scores, for instance—were trumpeted, often to suggest that desegregation was damaging educational standards for whites, sometimes to suggest the intellectual inferiority of blacks, or both. African-Americans, on the other hand, were affronted by the white assumption that the educational performances of black children should automatically improve as they took seats beside white children in desegregated classrooms.

Not just in the South but across the nation, busing brought out the most passionate opposition and turned dormant white reservations about desegregation into open resistance. Whites had not anticipated busing or "race mixing" or "forced integration" when they grudgingly accepted court-ordered school desegregation. Most probably had thought that a handful of exceptional black children, perhaps chosen by white school boards and officials, would be allowed to join white pupils in virtually all-white schools.* However loudly some whites might call for a color-blind society, white parents clearly did not want color-blind schools, especially if busing was to be the instrument for achieving them.

Amid increasing animosities the drive for integration ultimately had to give way. A later Supreme Court decision, *Milliken* v. *Bradley* (1974), discouraged desegregation policies that involved moving children across school district lines. Thereafter, poor districts, of which the poorest usually consisted of concentrations of minorities, got poorer. Affluent, mostly white districts opposed sharing or shifting resources, arguing that children in their own districts would suffer.

Following the election of Ronald Reagan in 1980, federal policies reduced funds for desegregation efforts and even encouraged court action to *end* successful desegregation programs, with administration officials piously maintaining that these programs no longer were needed since desegregation had been achieved.

In fact, in 1984 a typical black student in Chicago attended a school in which only 9 percent of the pupils were white; Detroit was as bad, as was Newark, and the white percentage in New York was only 11. It was 16 in Baltimore and 17 in Philadelphia but rose to the hardly magnificent level of 32 in Boston and Cincinnati and 35 in Milwaukee.

In 1968, 73.6 percent of black pupils, nationwide, had been in predominantly minority schools. Sixteen years later, in 1984, that percentage had fallen only to 63.5—and 33.2 percent of black pupils were in schools whose populations were *90 to 100 percent* composed of minorities.

So much for the "integration" of public schools by 1984, forty years after *Brown* v. *Board*—except in the South, "the Sahara of the Bozart," where in Louisville, Kentucky, a typical black pupil

---

*In Winston-Salem, North Carolina, where I was working as a reporter, that's exactly what happened in 1957. School officials selected three promising black pupils from willing families and admitted them to the formerly all-white R. J. Reynolds High School. Other schools in the city remained segregated.

attended a school that was 65 percent white, or Greensboro, North Carolina (the city in which the lunch counter sit-ins began, seemingly aeons ago), where a typical black pupil was in a school nearly 58 percent white.

Nor have things changed much since then. In 1992 a Harvard study found that 66 percent of African-American public school pupils still were attending schools with enrollment of more than 50 percent blacks or Latinos or both. Public schools across the nation, the survey found, were *more* segregated than they had been since 1967, a quarter century earlier.

By the autumn of 1995, a renewed campaign to end federal school desegregation initiatives, particularly busing, was flourishing nationwide, to the point that Gary Orfield of Harvard, an outspoken proponent of integration, conceded, "It's real, it's large and it's threatening to get us to a level of segregation we haven't seen since before the civil rights movement."

Among major cities questioning school desegregation in one way or another are Denver, Minneapolis, Cleveland, Pittsburgh, Seattle, Wilmington, Delaware, and Indianapolis. Norfolk and Oklahoma City already have quashed busing for the purpose of school desegregation. The rise of political conservatism and the consequent decline of liberalism, widespread public concern about the quality of public schools, and a series of Supreme Court decisions, dating to *Milliken* v. *Bradley* in 1974, have combined to bring about the renewed assault on busing and desegregation.[2]

Those who thought the race problem in America had been settled by civil rights legislation were abruptly disabused by the race riots of the late sixties, in Los Angeles, Chicago, Newark, Detroit—all across America. These urban upheavals, the Kerner Commission was to learn, were caused by blacks erupting in fury and despair against a range of inner-city grievances—poor housing, little police protection, no jobs—largely unnoticed or unadmitted by comfortable whites.

The riots ultimately flamed out, but not the black resentments they had reflected or the white fear and anger they had aroused. It was against a background of burning cities that George Wallace waged his backlash presidential campaign of 1968; Richard Nixon won the White House that same year with a less inflammatory appeal directed more subtly to alarmed whites.

Not long thereafter, in 1969, the affirmative action efforts of the Johnson administration were extended in Nixon's Philadelphia Plan, aimed at increasing economic opportunity for blacks. Nixon and the Republicans of his day preferred that course to the Democrats' sponsorship of civil rights legislation.

Labor opposed the Philadelphia Plan, often fiercely, since it was aimed at that city's lily-white construction unions. Labor was a vital element of the Democratic party, so Democrats, despite their supposed support for affirmative action, were none too enthusiastic either, particularly since Nixon had stolen some of their liberal thunder. That opened one of the first visible gaps between what had been cooperating liberal groups—in this case, organized labor and African-Americans.

The bitter pill of economic competition also was added to an already bubbling cauldron of racial animosities; blacks had never before seemed threatening as competitors. Now skilled white hard hats, it was supposed in country club locker rooms and working-class bowling alleys alike, were being forced to give up good jobs to unqualified blacks.

"Quotas" became a divisive issue, not only in employment but in college and professional school admissions. Jews, remembering when they had been *limited* by quotas for all sorts of educational and economic opportunities, feared that a revival of quotas, even if designed only to *benefit* blacks, might have the practical effect of once again excluding Jews. Another gap in liberal ranks had begun to open, this one between African-Americans and the Jews who had so strongly supported the civil rights movement.

In large part, however, the animosity of white persons of whatever class or ethnic group toward affirmative action was based on fear rather than fact. No white who actually lost or failed to get a job or who was excluded from educational opportunity because of affirmative action could be expected to be happy about it, but "quotas" in most cases really were "goals"—and justified goals at that.

If blacks were, say, 10 percent of a community's population, what was unfair or un-American about their having something like 10 percent of public, tax-financed jobs or of jobs controlled by unions that worked on public projects? Especially when African-Americans had for so long been unfairly deprived of any of such jobs? Why should not publicly supported institutions seek out for admission a fair proportion of blacks—or women, or any other previously excluded group?

In fact, despite various private and governmental efforts, including affirmative action in jobs and education, by the nineties not a lot of progress had been made against race and sex discrimination in American business and industry. In March 1995 the so-called Glass Ceiling Commission reported that white men, while only 43 percent of the work force, occupied about 95 of every 100 senior management positions, defined as vice-presidents and above.

Blacks and women clearly aren't very powerful competitors at that level. White women do hold about 40 percent of middle management jobs (officer managers, etc.), but blacks are still out of the game. Black women are about 5 percent of middle management jobholders; black men about 4 percent.[3]

Throughout the work force, at any level, it's hard to find support for the white males who claim they're now suffering discrimination. A study by Lee Badgett and Heidi Hartmann found no black gains made at the expense of "firm competitiveness or fair employment practices" and concluded that "many of the jobs gained by minorities and women" recently were new jobs, not those of displaced white males.[4] Similarly, Alfred W. Rosenblum, of the law faculty at Rutgers University, found that "reverse discrimination" cases accounted for only 1 to 3 percent of about three thousand reported employment discrimination cases in the four years 1990–94, and many of these were brought by disappointed job seekers who were found by the courts to be less qualified than the job winners.[5]

Of racial discrimination charges received by the Equal Employment Opportunity Commission, only 1.7 percent have been made by white males. On the other side of the coin, affirmative action has had some clear benefits for African-Americans—an increase, for example, from about 23,000 to more than 60,000 police officers in the years 1970–90. In the private sector in the same years the number of black pharmacists grew from 2,501 to 7,011.[6]

Racial inequality in employment, however, still is rampant in America. In the reasonably typical city of Indianapolis in 1991, 213,623 white persons working for the 1,107 largest private employers had an outsize advantage in job status over the 33,411 African-Americans working for the same concerns. Whites held a stunning share of places in each of the more desirable job categories: officials and managers 93.5 percent, professionals 92.7, technicians 86.6, sales workers 88, office and clerical workers 82.3, craftworkers 91.3.

The highest African-American share in any of these categories was 16.3 percent (office and clerical workers). About a third of all the African-Americans were either laborers or service workers.[7] White males are not complaining that these jobs have been taken away from them by "reverse discrimination."

Almost as soon as affirmative action was launched as a policy by the Johnson and Nixon administrations, it became in white eyes a grievance rather than the intended remedy for injustice to blacks. Neither facts nor logic have changed that view; in the nineties the grievance still festers, more hurtfully than ever.

In the last days of a 1990 election for the U.S. Senate in North Carolina, polls showed that an African-American Democrat, Harvey Gantt, was running well ahead of the incumbent, the "hard right" Republican Jesse Helms. Could Helms, whom North Carolina had elected three times despite his notoriously racist record, actually be defeated by a black man in a once-segregated southern state? It seemed possible; Gantt had consistently led in the polls while Helms stayed in Washington on Senate business.

In late October, however, virtually at the last minute, Helms came back to the state and drenched North Carolina's airwaves and households in a television commercial showing a pair of white hands tearing up a rejection slip for a job. The sound track made clear that the job had been given to a black, and almost without further effort Jesse Helms came from behind to win a fourth term.

The white hands spot, surely one of the most effective campaign ads ever filmed, had made all the difference. That was not lost on other politicians, and denunciations of affirmative action continued to be used by Republicans and some Democrats as political kindling, often without reference to facts.

It was not, however, until the triumph of Newt Gingrich and Republican conservatism in the 1994 House races that the issue flared again, even more hotly, into national prominence. Gingrich did not include opposition to affirmative action in his Contract with America, but the revanchist spirit of the document and the GOP campaign obviously encouraged foes of "reverse racism."

In January 1995 a poll by the *Wall Street Journal* and NBC showed 68 percent of white males and 61 percent of all adults in favor of "eliminating affirmative action based on race or gender." Only 28 percent of white males and 32 percent of all adults opposed that rather tricky idea. Had the question been one of "eliminating affirmative action to provide equal opportunity for all Americans," the response might have been somewhat different. In fact, the Supreme Court had long since ruled out preference by "race or gender"; it has decreed that these elements can only be *one factor* in a selection process.

In July 1995, in a poll taken for *USA Today* and the Cable News Network, one question was whether affirmative action should be reformed or eliminated. Of white respondents, 60 percent favored reform and only 24 percent opted for elimination. Moreover, 53 percent of whites thought affirmative action had been good for the country; 37 percent thought not. Black respondents were predictably more favorable to affirmative action.

Senator Joseph Lieberman, the new chairman of the Democratic Leadership Council, of which Bill Clinton once was the leader, struck an early blow at affirmative action when he told questioners at the National Press Club in Washington that "preferential policies" based on race or sex were patently unfair.

"You can't defend policies that are based on group preferences as opposed to individual opportunities, which is what America has always been about," Lieberman said.[8] That would be news to the millions of African-Americans who suffered both as a group and as individuals for centuries of preferences for whites as well as to the many individual women and individual blacks who benefited later from affirmative action programs.

Lieberman appeared to raise the possibility of Democratic backsliding on affirmative action; that appearance was heightened when Stanley Greenberg, Clinton's preferred poll taker, warned that "the Democratic coalition cannot be based on social justice claims of some segment of their coalition against other segments of the coalition. . . ."[9]

Governor Pete Wilson of California became a Republican presidential candidate early in 1995, after having won reelection in 1994; later in the year, having generated little support, he withdrew from the presidential race. Wilson became the first sizable political figure to exploit revived public hostility to affirmative action—and in the process furthered the revival. Having been reelected largely owing to his stand in favor of Proposition 187—to deny welfare and other social benefits to illegal immigrants—Wilson announced that he would support a ballot proposition in 1996 to bar the state of California from awarding jobs or contracts on the basis of race or sex. That's the way opponents characterize affirmative action, despite the Supreme Court.

In July 1995 Wilson lent powerful support when the Board of Regents of the University of California voted, 14–10, to discontinue the use of race, sex, religion, color, or national origin as criteria for admission to the university. The board then approved, 15–10, similar restrictions on university hiring and contracting. Most of the regents had been appointed by Wilson or his Republican predecessor as governor, George Deukmejian.

These steps were taken in a highly charged atmosphere and

despite opposition picketers, an impassioned appeal by Jesse Jackson, warnings that Wilson's political intrusion into the university's affairs would damage its educational standing, and predictions that admissions of even academically qualified blacks would fall by 40 to 50 percent and that of qualified Hispanics by 5 to 15 percent. On the other hand, studies showed, admissions of Asians, many of whom excel academically, would rise while white enrollments would remain about the same.

In fact, in 1994 black enrollment in the University of California was still only 4 percent of the total, and it had not risen at all since 1984. In the same ten years Hispanic enrollment jumped from 7 to 13 percent, and that of Asians from 16 to 29 percent.

Even before California acted, President Clinton had ordered a federal review of affirmative action programs—not necessarily to revoke them but ostensibly to weigh their merits against frequent public complaints. His order may have had the effect on the general public of counterbalancing Governor Wilson, a potential presidential rival. It also evoked considerable African-American outrage.

"I do not support wide-ranging, ill-defined reviews," declared Maxine Waters, the fiery congresswoman from California. "All this talk about 'reviews' signals that perhaps something is wrong and needs to be 'fixed.' "[10]

Her and other blacks' alarm proved unfounded or else had powerful effect on Clinton. On July 19 he gave a clear endorsement to affirmative action, canceled no program that had been reviewed, ordered no drastic revisions, denied that affirmative action was no longer needed, and emphasized the obvious: "The job of ending discrimination in this country is not over."

Senator Bob Dole of Kansas, the Republican majority leader and in 1995 the front-runner for the Republican presidential nomination, had followed Pete Wilson's lead with a pledge to end preferences for women and minorities—despite his having once been the prime sponsor of the Glass Ceiling Commission.

Dole told the Senate: "After nearly thirty years of government-sanctioned quotas, time tables, set-asides, and other racial preferences, the American people sense all too clearly that the race-counting game has gone too far."[11]

This was a remarkable statement. Dole had sponsored not only the Glass Ceiling Commission but also one of the "preference programs" he now pledged to kill, and he himself acknowledged that racial and sex discrimination was still a problem in the United States.

The Supreme Court has not remained silent. On April 17, 1995, the justices refused to review a lower-court ruling that race-based promotions were unfair to white firefighters in Birmingham, Alabama. That was not actual approval of the lower-court decision, but it was not a reversal either—not even of the strong language in which the appeals court denounced the Birmingham plan as "the perpetuation of discrimination by government." Yet the plan had achieved its goal of promoting black *and* white firefighters on a one-to-one basis until the number of black lieutenants equaled the black percentage of the surrounding county's work force. No white firefighters had lost their jobs, and most promotions for whites were delayed only for a few months.

Later the High Court invalidated a University of Maryland scholarship program designed for blacks and intended to counter the university's long history of racial discrimination, which had lasted into the eighties. That intent apparently made no difference to the justices in the majority, nor did it seem to matter that the Clinton administration supported the university.

On June 12 the High Court struck even harder at affirmative action. In a five to four decision the Court declared that only those federal programs that could withstand "strict scrutiny" were constitutional; previously this restrictive doctrine had been applied only to *state* programs. "Strict scrutiny" means that courts must find programs "narrowly tailored" to achieve "a compelling government interest." Justice Thurgood Marshall once wrote that such a standard is "strict in theory but fatal in fact" to programs subjected to it.

Justice Sandra Day O'Connor's decision, however, did not rule out affirmative action programs entirely; rather she brought their constitutionality into considerable doubt. Specifically, the federal highway contract at issue in *Adarand* v. *Pena* was sent back to a lower court for "strict scrutiny." For its survival, elaborate proof would have to be adduced that minorities had been systematically excluded from specific markets. The generalized history of discrimination against minority firms would not be sufficient.

The *Adarand* decision, said Clint Bolick, the litigation director for the Washington-based Institute of Justice, meant that "the era of racial preferences is finally coming to an end. . . . It's really the Court saying 'enough is enough.'" But affirmative action supporters, perhaps whistling past the graveyard, refused to call the decision a disaster. None claimed, however, that it *improved* the outlook for minority firms to get federal contracts, although only 6 percent of those contracts now go to businesses owned by minorities or women.

Several important African-American voices were heard on both sides of the issue in 1995. One was that of Colin Powell, who had scrupulously maintained public silence on most political issues, despite pressures on him to run for the presidency. He was overheard, however, by a New York *Daily News* editorial writer, Jonathan Capehart, as Powell *supported* affirmative action in a speech at a boys' school in Newark.

Powell's spokesman argued that the speech was intended to be private, but Capehart quoted the general anyway: "The notion that affirmative action should be completely stripped away [is] ridiculous. Anyone who would suggest that racism is a thing of the past is wrong. People are still being denied access to jobs because of the color of their skin."*

This statement as quoted set Powell at odds with Ward Connerly, an African-American regent at the University of California. Connerly had pushed hard for the vote to end affirmative

---

*Powell's spokesman did not deny but would not confirm this statement. The general also said, according to Capehart: "I don't want someone to give me a job just because I'm black."

action, on the ground that such programs had outlived their usefulness.

Glenn Loury, the Boston College economist, wrote in a *New York Times* op-ed article on July 26, 1995, that "affirmative action retards the attainment" of Martin Luther King's "vision of universal brotherhood and equality before God" and King's belief that "racial identity has no moral significance."

Harvard sociologist Orlando Patterson took the opposite tack in a later *Times* op-ed piece (August 7). He wrote that it would be "hard to find a program that has brought so much gain to so many at so little cost." Affirmative action, in Patterson's judgment, "has been the single most important factor in the rise of a significant, if still economically fragile, black middle class."

The intellectual scholar Shelby Steele,[12] in an earlier *Times* op-ed article, had denounced affirmative action but added an important corollary that Wilson and other critics have not specified. Steele advocated that "discrimination by race, gender or ethnicity be a criminal offense"—a felony, in fact. "If someone can go to jail for stealing my car stereo, he ought to do considerably more time for stifling my livelihood and well-being by discriminating against me."

Steele was eloquent on his view of affirmative action as an indignity to blacks and a cause of hypocrisy in whites. But neither he nor Bob Dole, who also demanded tough enforcement of antidiscrimination laws, noted that the Equal Employment Opportunities Commission, which is charged with that duty, has an overwhelming backlog of cases, so many that it may never be able to decide them all. If enforcement of antidiscrimination laws is the alternative to affirmative action, race, sex, and ethnic discrimination will be with us for a long time.

8 Majority and Minority

You can't draw districts without taking race into account.

Justice David Souter

If Louisiana decided to draw a district for Creoles, that would not trigger a Constitutional challenge.

Drew S. Days III,
U.S. solicitor general[1]

In 1992 North Carolina elected two black members of Congress, the first of their race to serve in the House of Representatives from that state since the Reconstruction era that followed the Civil War. Owing to reapportionment in other states following the 1990 census, a record number of African-American members of Congress also were elected that year. Black membership in the House rose from twenty-six to thirty-nine.

In 1995, however, a Supreme Court mostly appointed by Presidents Reagan and Bush struck down Georgia's Eleventh Congressional District, specially drawn by the state legislature to include a majority of African-Americans. In doing so, the

Court ruled that any legislative district created by any state with race as a "predominant factor" should be presumed unconstitutional.

That decision and others issued on the final day of the Court's 1994–95 term left many questions unanswered, particularly how judges are to decide whether race was predominant in the drawing of the boundaries of a district. No one could doubt, however, that the decision in the Georgia case opened to legal challenge most of the redistricting plans that had sharply increased black— and doubled minority—representation in the House in 1992.

The irony was cruel. In approximately two centuries since the founding of the Republic, blacks continually had suffered crippling political discrimination and lack of representation, particularly but not exclusively in the South. Then, in 1992, more than a century after the Emancipation Proclamation, for the first time since post–Civil War Reconstruction, black representation in the House, from North Carolina, the South, and the nation, moved toward, though not all the way to, proportional equality with that of whites.

Whereupon whites, most of whom had never concerned themselves with the centuries-old lack of representation for blacks, claimed to be the innocent victims of discrimination! And the highest court in the land appeared to uphold them.

The Georgia ruling left many questions unanswered because Justice Anthony Kennedy's decision was unduly vague and because, on the same day, the Supreme Court, without comment and in an unsigned order, upheld a 1992 redistricting plan in which California had created nine new majority-black and majority-Hispanic districts, though these also had been challenged by white voters. The Court also announced that day that in its next term it would hear and decide two more redistricting cases, from North Carolina and Texas.

The California decision indicated that race could be at least one—though the Georgia ruling held that it could not be the predominant—factor in drawing district lines. So did Justice Sandra Day O'Connor, a member of the majority, in a concurring decision. The others voting to uphold the majority ruling were Chief Justice William Rehnquist and Justices Antonin Scalia and Clarence Thomas.

What differentiated, in their minds, the Georgia from the California case? And if the one was considered to rely more upon race than the other, how was that determined, and how will the question be decided in the North Carolina and Texas cases yet to be heard and in others from other states that probably will reach the Supreme Court?

No clear answers were available in the wake of the Georgia case, but the recent judicial record made it clear that a narrow majority of the Court was antipathetic to so-called racial preferences and thus to so-called majority-minority districts—those drawn primarily to elect African-Americans or Hispanics (as in the Texas case yet to be decided).

Together Presidents Reagan and Bush had appointed at least a fluctuating conservative majority on the Supreme Court on which Earl Warren and Thurgood Marshall once sat. When Bush left office in 1993, moreover, he and Reagan had appointed more than half of all federal judges then serving at any level.*

The Reagan-Bush Supreme Court (as recounted in Chapter Seven) ruled against the University of Maryland's scholarship program for blacks, refused to review a lower court's invalidation of a Birmingham plan to promote black firefighters, and cast considerable doubt on the constitutionality of all affirmative action programs. The Court's ruling in the Georgia districting case continued the obvious trend.

The Reagan-Bush Court's antagonistic attitude toward "preferences" had been suggested even earlier by its June 1993 order

---

*Only a "fluctuating" majority dominated the Supreme Court because David Souter, Bush's appointee, proved to be a less predictable "conservative" than expected. See Chapter Thirteen for an example. Some court watchers, not including the author, regard Justice O'Connor as also a "fluctuating" conservative.

in *Shaw* v. *Reno* for reconsideration of a district court's approval of the newly drawn Twelfth Congressional District of North Carolina. And the wording of the decision—written by Justice O'Connor, a Reagan appointee and, as the first woman on the Court, arguably the beneficiary of a sexual preference—rubbed salt in the wound.

Her decision angered liberals, African-Americans, and others, but the substance of the ruling was widely acclaimed as a reassertion of democratic values over "reverse discrimination" and ancient gerrymandering standards seldom before restricted by legal action. Thus *Shaw* v. *Reno* clearly foreshadowed the later, more restrictive Georgia ruling, and its reasoning told much about the Court's attitude toward racial preference and majority-minority legislative districts.

Undeniably the Twelfth North Carolina* was bizarrely drawn, more so than Georgia's Eleventh. The Twelfth stretched along Interstate 85 for more than a hundred miles, at some points not much wider than the highway, looking on a map rather like a wriggling snake but taking in parts of most of North Carolina's urban centers, from Durham through Greensboro and Winston-Salem to Charlotte.

Nobody denied that the Twelfth was drawn to include areas where many of the state's African-Americans resided, though the motives of the drawers were and still are disputed. Were Bush administration officials, who urged the state to create two majority-minority districts, concerned for racial representation? Or were they actually trying to concentrate black voters so that other districts would be more white and more Republican?

At any rate, the racial makeup of the Twelfth, about 53 percent black to 47 percent white, made likely the election of an

---

*The following discussion of majority-minority districts in the South has been informed by *Redistricting and Representation*, a research paper by David A. Bositis of the Joint Center for Political and Economic Studies in Washington. Opinions and conclusions, however, are those of the author.

African-American member of Congress.* And in 1992 the Twelfth did elect one of North Carolina's two black members of the House of Representatives, the first of their race to represent the state in the "hall of the people" in *more than a century*.

That met the ostensible goal of the Bush administration's Justice Department. Taking their text from language a Democratic Congress had written into the Voting Rights Act, Justice Department officials in 1990 had required the North Carolina legislature to "avoid the dilution of black voting strength" when it drew new district lines based on 1990 census results.

Those results showed that 22 percent of North Carolina's voting-age population was African-American. These blacks were not so concentrated in one area, however, or even two, as to set up one or two natural congressional districts in which blacks would be in the majority or have a plausible chance to elect one of their own. Since African-Americans nevertheless were more than a fifth of the population of a state whose total population entitled it to twelve seats in the House, the Justice Department argued that blacks were entitled to two of the seats.

Was an undemocratic and impermissible "preference" therefore handed to African-Americans?

Hardly. The *real* preference had been claimed by southern whites, practically though not legally, during the long decades when black representation in Congress, particularly from the old Confederate states, certainly from North Carolina, hardly existed.

Even in 1992, twenty-seven years after first passage of the Voting Rights Act, five southern states other than North Carolina had *no* black members of Congress, and each of the six had a black voting-age population (BVAP) exceeding 20 percent of the total state population. In that year even in the five southern states where black members of Congress *had* been elected (Georgia, Louisiana, Mississippi, Tennessee, and Texas), the black pro-

---

*The district is described in the past tense since at the time of writing and in view of the Georgia ruling it seemed unlikely that it ultimately could survive judicial scrutiny.

portion of each state's congressional delegation was substantially *less* than the BVAP's share of total population.

Southern congressional districts, however, had to be redrawn for the 1992 midterm elections, following the 1990 census. That resulted in North Carolina's Twelfth (and Georgia's Eleventh), among other majority-minority districts. In 1992, as a result, blacks were elected in 17, or 13.6 percent, of 125 southern congressional districts—scarcely a revolution but a substantial change nevertheless. These black members of Congress *still* represented only 41.8 percent of eligible black voters in the South, in six southern states more black voters remained represented by white Democrats than by blacks, and in a predictive sign for the future, in South Carolina more black voters were represented by white *Republicans* than by either white or black Democrats.

Thus, even with the inclusion of North Carolina's Twelfth and other majority-minority districts, 58.2 percent of the South's black voters continued to be represented by whites. In North Carolina itself, though 43 percent of black voters lived in the two new districts represented by blacks, 57 percent still were represented by whites.

These southern elections, however, were a major reason for the increase from 26 to 39 African-American members of Congress in 1993. Again, this was hardly a revolution. Blacks are about 12 percent of the national population, and 39 was less than 10 percent of the 439 members of the House. But the change was more significant than the numbers suggested.

An enlarged Congressional Black Caucus gained more influence within the controlling (as it was then) Democratic party and thus within the House itself. Increased numbers of black southern legislators could more effectively influence southern white legislators, particularly if they were Democrats, to pay attention to the interests of their black constituents. In many white-represented districts, a significant proportion of the constituency was black, and those black voters could be expected in most cases to be responsive to the views of elected black representatives from other districts and to compare them with the votes of their white representatives.

*   *   *

Justice O'Connor's decision in *Shaw* v. *Reno* was almost as bizarre as the Twelfth District itself. The decision declared, for one thing, that the district's outlines violated the color-blind standards of "a political system in which race no longer matters." As if race had *not* mattered in America, beyond most other considerations, before and since the Declaration of Independence! As if a few laws and a few decisions by O'Connor's predecessors had overruled history and ingrained American attitudes to create a system in which "race no longer mattered"! As if somehow a "color-blind" society actually had existed, and still did exist, and African-Americans were brazenly claiming a racial preference contrary to all American experience!

O'Connor also wrote that the Voting Rights Act and the Twelfth District were creating "an uncomfortable resemblance to political apartheid." That was a truly astounding charge against a law and one of its consequences, both of which had been aimed at rectifying the deepest injustices of American history, a law that already had resulted in the vote for millions previously cheated of it, a consequence that in one year had increased African-American representation in the House of Representatives by 50 percent—but still not to proportional equality.

The charge was neither tactful nor factually sound, even in regard to the oddly shaped Twelfth District. The black-white population ratio there was 53 to 47—*not* overwhelmingly black and well within the two-party definition of a competitive district: one usually or typically carried with less than 55 percent of the vote. Could the Twelfth be won by a white? Depending on the vagaries of personality, issues, money, and campaigning, yes; a strong white candidate would have a reasonable chance to defeat a weak black candidate, a far better chance, on the record, than a minority candidate in a white-majority district.

Two Hispanic-majority districts in the South already have elected non-Hispanic white members of Congress. For years a southern black-majority district regularly returned Representative Lindy Boggs, a white woman from New Orleans. On the other hand, of 101 white-majority districts in the South, *none* has a minority representative; most southern black voters continue to be represented in the House by whites, including white Republicans.

In fact, if any apartheid was involved, it was not in the southern majority-minority districts. They were the most racially *diverse* in the South: On average, black-majority districts in the region were only 55 percent black, Hispanic-majority districts only 62 percent Hispanic, but white-majority districts were *83 percent white*.

Aside from its semantic excess and factual ignorance, O'Connor's opinion did raise real and difficult questions, first and foremost of which was familiar from the long affirmative action debate: Is it proper and constitutionally permissible to seek to rectify a proved racial disadvantage by granting an admitted racial preference?

Those who demand (or, more often, proclaim) a color-blind society in which any preference for anybody is supposedly ruled out seemed—like Sandra Day O'Connor and the four members of her majority—to have the Constitution on their side. Those who were not offended by racial preference to remedy racial discrimination, on the other hand, seemed to be arguing that what blacks and liberals had so long opposed—racial discrimination—was permissible if directed against whites rather than blacks and for a good purpose.

These were easy, though widespread, assumptions. But in the first place, as demonstrated above, no certain preference for African-Americans had been granted in the creation of North Carolina's Twelfth District, a mere 53–47 black-majority congressional district—not in a state with a 22 percent BVAP, twelve seats in Congress, and *no* black occupying any of them for more than a century.

In the second place, even if that district did or potentially could represent a preference for blacks, a disadvantage for blacks deliberately created or tacitly condoned by whites could be overcome only by a countervailing preference *for* blacks. If the discrimination against blacks were merely forbidden for the future, with no remedial action for the past, not only might the dis-crimination continue clandestinely—especially in the case of southern congressional districts—but the political disadvantage accumulated in the years of discrimination would not have been redressed.

An analogy: If a teller who had been embezzling from a bank were caught and stopped but not made to restore the bank's losses, the bank would not really have had its grievance reme-died. Or as Federal District Judge Stanley Sporkin put it in dismissing an out-of-court settlement in a case involving the Mi-crosoft Corporation, "Simply telling a defendant to go forth and sin no more does little or nothing to redress the unfair advantage it has already gained."

In the third place—no less important than the first two—a preference to overcome admitted past racial discrimination is *not* a new form of an old unconstitutional practice. It's racial prej-udice and discrimination in pursuit of it that are unconstitu-tional. When whites prevented blacks from voting, as no one denies that they did, that was unconstitutional racial discrimi-nation. But there's no intent to discriminate racially against whites when the law upholds blacks' right to vote or to be po-litically represented, and any resulting loss of political power or convenience by whites is incidental to, not the unconstitutional purpose of, addressing the compelling societal need of undoing discrimination against African-Americans.

The hundreds of years of discrimination against blacks (eco-nomic, social, political), moreover, actually had resulted over those years in numerous racial preferences *for whites*—in jobs or college admissions or better rest rooms or major-league baseball contracts or many other desirable assets that blacks had not been allowed to have, for which they often had not even been allowed to apply. Against these real and centuries-old preferences *for* whites—what is it but a job or admissions preference if only whites are permitted to apply or if only whites can be hired or admitted?—almost no one, including those who, following de-segregation, most stridently denounced "reverse discrimination," had raised objections.

Other questions were raised by *Shaw* v. *Reno*. Could American citizens be adequately represented in Congress if they had not the numerical strength in a given district to elect one of their own race? The barely outnumbered white voters who brought suit against the Twelfth District essentially argued that they could not be adequately represented in such circumstances, and the Supreme Court seemed by five to four to consider the question arguable.

Before the 1992 redistricting, however, North Carolina's African-Americans, a fifth of the state's population in 1990, did not have the numerical strength in any district to elect one of their own. They had had to be satisfied with whatever representation white members of Congress chose to give them. Was it fairer to let that continue or to take political action to provide an opportunity—not necessarily a certainty—for blacks to elect one or more black members of Congress? Was "reverse discrimination" against Twelfth District whites, if it existed, more reprehensible or less constitutional than the direct discrimination blacks had suffered for so long? Which more nearly presented "an uncomfortable resemblance to political apartheid"?

O'Connor also called it a "crude and impermissible" stereotype to hold that "members of the same racial group, regardless of their age, education, economic status, or the community in which they live, think alike, share the same political interests, and will prefer the same candidates at the polls."

Of course they don't—not necessarily. But it's hardly stereotypical thinking to believe that an African-American member of Congress might have a greater understanding of some problems peculiar to blacks, just as a woman often understands the problems of other women better than a man would. Did O'Connor ask whether women "regardless of their age, education, economic status, or the community in which they live" would feel adequately represented politically if all members of Congress were male? Or if the abortion issue were to be decided exclusively by males?

*   *   *

If the drawing of majority-minority districts after 1990 was proper and justified, however, it was not without political cost to African-Americans. The new majority-minority districts actually may have represented an indirect new *limitation* on African-American political power, seeming clearly, for example, to some extent responsible for the Democrats' loss of control of the House in 1994.

The Republican takeover, that is, was greatly aided by the GOP's gain of sixteen seats in the South, all of which had been occupied by white Democrats, all of which were won by white Republicans. For the first time in history a *Republican majority* of southern members of Congress was elected in 1994. A crucial factor was the shift of many southern black voters into majority-minority districts.

That shift had increased African-American numerical strength in the House in 1992 and helped maintain it in 1994, when all southern black members (except Craig Washington of Texas, who was replaced by a black woman, Sheila Jackson Lee) were returned. But the shift also resulted in *fewer black voters in white-majority districts*, hence an improved Republican chance to carry them, particularly in 1994, a Republican year anyway.

From 1982 to 1990, with districts drawn in response to the 1980 census, the Democrats remained easily the dominant party in southern House delegations. But the 1990 census and the resulting reapportionment brought an average six percentage point decline in the Democratic vote in white-majority districts in 1992, a decline that roughly matched the average five percentage point decline in the BVAP in those districts. Those black voters had been switched to the new majority-minority districts.

In 1994 a more severe blow fell on the Democrats: Their vote in white-majority districts in the South declined from 49 to 38 percent of the total, mostly because the unpopular Clinton administration's drag on Democratic candidates in 1994 was greater than the drag of unpopular George Bush atop the Republican ticket in 1992.

*   *   *

Returns from Georgia show what happened in one southern state and suggest the ill effect on the Democratic party in all, perhaps also on African-Americans of the majority-minority districts.

Before the reapportionment for 1992, Georgia's ten-seat House delegation was composed of eight white Democrats, one black Democrat, and one white Republican, Newt Gingrich. The eight white Democrats' districts had 70.7 percent of the BVAP, the one black Democrat represented 21.3 of Georgia's black voters, mostly in Atlanta, and Gingrich had the remaining 8 percent (he had been only narrowly reelected in 1990).

The 1992 reapportionment (based on the 1990 census) reflected population growth that entitled Georgia to an eleventh seat in Congress. The Democrats in control of state government, under black and Bush administration pressures, drew up two new majority-minority districts (including the Eleventh), in addition to the existing Atlanta black-majority district; the two new and the one old districts together contained *61.7 percent* of Georgia's black voters.

These districts duly returned three black members of Congress in 1992, all Democrats, but the consolidation of black voters into just three districts helped Republicans to take over three seats in other districts that were "whiter" than they otherwise would have been. Gingrich also was reelected; so in the 103d Congress (1993–95) Georgia's delegation included four white Republicans, three black Democrats, and only four white Democrats.

As noted, the anti-Democratic trend worsened in the House elections of 1994. White Republicans captured *three more* formerly white Democratic seats—primarily because of the ill repute in which the Democratic party and the Clinton administration were held in the South, but not least because 61.7 percent of Georgia's black voters had been concentrated in only three districts. So the Georgia delegation for the 1995–97 congressional session consists of seven white Republicans, three black Democrats, and only one white Democrat—an astounding party and racial change in just four years.

The white Republicans, including Gingrich, now represent 37

percent of Georgia's BVAP; the one white Democrat's district has only 1.3 percent. The 1992 and 1994 returns in Georgia and other southern states suggest that clustering black, mostly Democratic voters in majority-minority districts, consequently leaving greater white majorities in other districts, cost the Democratic party as many as five seats in 1992 and another five in 1994.

Mere numbers are not the only relevant measure of this development. As already noted, the Congressional Black Caucus, though it maintained its numerical membership, became a minority within a minority, had to give up numerous committee and subcommittee posts and staff positions, and generally lost a good deal of "clout" for the 104th Congress.

The Republicans and the Bush Department of Justice apparently foresaw this possibility and that of Republican gains in the South; otherwise they hardly would have pushed southern Democratic governors and legislatures, as they did, to create more majority-minority districts likely to go Democratic. As anticipated, the surrounding districts became "whiter," which in the South these days means more Republican and more competitive between the two parties.

Nevertheless, the Republicans may suffer an unanticipated side effect of their own. Southern Republican members of Congress now represent 30.8 percent of southern black voters, a sharp increase from the 19.9 percent they represented after the 1992 election. For the first time these southern Republicans represent more black voters than do white southern Democrats. So it's plausible to ask what long-term impact substantial black minorities in Republican-represented districts may have on Republican voting patterns in the House.

Those minority voters also could be significant in districts where Republican victories were narrow in 1992 and 1994; twelve Republicans elected originally in those years won with less than 56 percent of the vote. They will be not only contested but *targeted* in 1996; knowing that, fearing defeat, they might feel a heightened need to respond to pressures from their black constituents.

*   *   *

The invalidation of Georgia's Eleventh District obviously left that state's legislature, controlled by Democrats, in a dilemma. Should it try to regain Democratic party dominance in the state's congressional delegation by returning substantial numbers of black voters to newly Republican districts? Would those blacks, in that event, remain faithful to a Democratic party that had sacrificed black representation in Congress to party power?

Or should Georgia's legislators continue to give blacks enlarged representation through majority-minority districts even at the expense of party interests? If so, how was it to be done without making race the "predominant factor" in drawing district lines, which the Supreme Court has forbidden? Or was there some formula to be found in the upholding of California's majority-minority districts that could be applied in Georgia?

Eventually, the Georgia legislature, after a twenty-day special session, defaulted on these difficult questions in September 1995. In December, a three-judge panel of the U.S. Court of Appeals for the Eleventh Circuit—two of whom had been appointed by Democrat Jimmy Carter—opted to scrap two of Georgia's majority-minority districts, redisperse its black voting-age population, and give Democrats—not surprisingly—a shot at recapturing several seats that had gone Republican in the recent past.

In doing so, the judges also forced two of Georgia's black representatives to compete in new districts, against incumbent white Republicans, in newly drawn districts with black voting-age populations of only 33 and 23 percent. These new districts are at least as solidly white-majority as the short-lived former districts were black-majority, if not more so.

The two judges in the majority asserted that their ruling was in accordance with the Supreme Court decree that black-majority districts could not be created if race was the dominant factor in the creation. The new plan left Georgia with only one black-majority district, in the Atlanta metropolitan area, represented by John Lewis. Whether the plan will be upheld after certain appeal remains to be seen, but previous Supreme Court decisions suggest it will be approved, despite the likely loss of black representation.

Similar problems will face other states that created majority-minority districts following the 1990 census. North Carolina's celebrated Twelfth, for example, is still disputed; after *Shaw* v. *Reno* returned it to the district court for reconsideration, that tribunal approved the district again, whereupon white voters appealed again. Then, as announced on the day of the Georgia ruling, the Supreme Court began to consider for a second time the long-disputed validity of the Twelfth District.

Only an optimist would predict its survival, but as Justice Ruth Bader Ginsburg pointedly observed in a dissent from the Georgia ruling, the Court has not spoken its "final word" in its inconclusive rulings on majority-minority districts. Despite its clear opposing trend, a new High Court opening, if filled by President Clinton, might reverse the five-to-four majority that struck down Georgia's Eleventh.

Meanwhile any candidate who loses an election in a legislative district with a majority not of his or her race—or in the drawing of whose boundaries "other factors carried less weight than race" (in Justice Ginsburg's words)—has a clear invitation to file suit and try to win in court what he or she could not at the polls.

That would be so not only in congressional but in state legislative, county commission, and city council districts. In the concentration of press and public on the smashing Republican congressional victory of 1994, it went largely unnoticed that African-American representation in southern legislative bodies also increased substantially, another result of redistricting on the basis of the 1990 census and under the influence of the Voting Rights Act.

In southern senates black members have increased by 155 percent, from 43 to 67; black representation in southern assemblies is up by 133 percent, from 159 members to 213. But the increase may be only temporary because many state legislative districts newly represented by blacks may be vulnerable to challenges based on the Georgia decision that race may not be the "predominant factor" in drawing district boundaries.

For the first time since Reconstruction, moreover, in 1994 Republicans won control of the lower houses in North and South Carolina and of the senate in Florida, perhaps the strongest evidence yet of an emerging Republican South. That too was partially the result of concentrating the previously dispersed African-American electorate. Thus southern state legislatures, paradoxically, are more black but also more Republican, perhaps posing again for Democratic legislators a difficult choice between party and black interests.

To African-Americans contemplating the Democrats' loss of power and influence in Congress—but unlikely to turn Republican in any great numbers—this may well suggest that the "continuing investment of all of black America's political capital in the Democratic party represents a rather large political risk."[2]

It represents a larger risk, surely, than that of moving "black America" toward the political party suggested earlier in these pages, a new party dedicated to economic, social, and political gains for the poor, particularly African-Americans.

Some, like Wade Henderson, the legal director of the NAACP, may see the invalidation of Georgia's Eleventh District as "the first step in the resegregation of American electoral democracy." Others, like Assistant Attorney General Deval L. Patrick, may consider that ruling "a setback . . . not the end of the road."[3]

It seems clear either way that African-Americans have a hard fight ahead if they are to gain and keep greater political representation in the legislative bodies of America.

9 "A Term Devoid of Hope"

I did not know that I would prove to be so correct.

Daniel P. Moynihan
(of his 1965 report on
the disintegration of the
black family)

Jean Harris, the former headmistress of the Madeira School in Virginia, spent twelve years in New York's Bedford Hills Correctional Facility after shooting her lover. A Phi Beta Kappa at Smith College, with a master's degree from Wayne State University, Ms. Harris, while at Bedford Hills, gathered the material for what she called "a Ph.D. in criminology."

Among the things she learned from other women in prison, mostly poor and many black, was that in America "hundreds of thousands of young mothers-to-be don't see a doctor until their baby is born."

As at least one result, many babies born in poverty also are born prematurely. Thereafter one out of every five such babies goes on to live in poverty. In a speech delivered after her release, Ms. Harris drew a blunt conclusion: "If you want a definition of very poor long-range planning and a recipe for more prisons and prisoners, there it is."[1]

*　　*　　*

The underclass first came to wide public notice in 1965, when President Johnson's White House released a study by Daniel Patrick Moynihan, then a Labor Department official, now the Democratic senior senator from New York. Moynihan's paper was entitled *The Negro Family: The Case for National Action.*

The study pointed out that despite the civil rights gains of the 1960s, "vast numbers of the unskilled, poorly educated city working class" of blacks were being left far behind economically and socially. But Moynihan properly placed most of the obloquy not on poor blacks but on "three centuries of sometimes unimaginable mistreatment [of] the Negro people."

Specifically he contended that slavery, segregation, and rising unemployment had undermined the role of the black male as family head and economic provider. With this traditional pillar of responsibility and discipline absent or diminished, Moynihan suggested, the black family had tended to disintegrate, leaving unemployment, divorce, abandonment, and illegitimacy prevalent in the inner city, and delinquency, crime, narcotics addiction, and educational failure on the rise.

Unfortunately, as is the case with most prescient insights and unwelcome revelations, Moynihan's dire portrait of what was in fact the emerging underclass inspired more outrage against *him* among those who might have been expected to respond most favorably—white liberals and blacks—than action against inner-city problems.

Liberals, largely ignoring the author's condemnation of centuries of black oppression, tended to see the Moynihan Report as an example of blaming the victim. The report also, and not unnaturally, ran afoul of the black pride sentiments then developing. Some thought it downgraded what had been accomplished by civil rights legislation. The report also piqued the latent guilt feelings of leaders of both races who had focused their efforts on civil rights and the South rather than on the inner city's economic and social problems (or pathologies, as Moynihan perhaps unfortunately termed them). And many antipathetic whites found in Moynihan's work confirmation of their belief that blacks were inherently inferior—or lazy or vicious or sexually irresponsible, or all of the above.

This hostile reaction undoubtedly held back both scholarly research into and public discussion of inner-city dynamics until an underclass explosion in the seventies forced the subject into public concern. Then and later it became clear that Moynihan had been right not only about the dissolution of the black family but about the impending inner-city crisis.

His study also had made clear that inner-city conditions were being forced by a history and by current problems over which blacks had little control, and this continued to be true as the underclass expanded. Prime among such societal, not just black, problems was unemployment; good jobs, particularly manufacturing jobs, were disappearing from the inner city, lost to relocated plants in the suburbs, the Sun Belt and overseas, to automation, to the shift to service rather than goods production.

Various studies have shown what happened to urban economies in the seventies and eighties. In the first of those crucial decades Boston, Chicago, Cleveland, New York, Detroit, and Philadelphia lost a *net* of about a half million jobs, and most of the jobs gained as replacements were in "knowledge-intensive" services, for which poor blacks usually were not qualified. In the same cities the number of jobs requiring less than a high school diploma *declined* by anywhere from 40 to 59 percent, while the number of jobs requiring at least some college education increased.

From 1967 to 1976 more than a million manufacturing, wholesale, and retail jobs, the kind best suited to most blacks of that era, disappeared from New York, Chicago, Philadelphia, and Detroit—in which cities, not incidentally, by 1982 more than a quarter of the nation's poor were living. Between 1979 and 1985, as if the loss of old jobs were not bad enough, nearly half of all *newly created* jobs paid no more than poverty-level wages.

In 1970 more than 40 percent of all employed black males in the ten largest cities held blue-collar jobs, compared with only 22 percent of employed whites. That made African-Americans disproportionately vulnerable to blue-collar decline. Still, by 1974, 48 percent of black males aged twenty to twenty-four had hung on to skilled or semiskilled industrial and craft jobs that paid enough for them to support a family. By 1986, twelve years later, only 25 percent of black males in that age-group had such jobs. And the wage stagnation of the seventies adversely affected even those who had managed to keep their old jobs.

In the manufacturing sector, which once had employed so many urban blacks:

> The combined shock of increased foreign competition, stagflation, and technological upgrading . . . has translated into massive unemployment, cutbacks, wage cuts and periodic layoffs—notably in older, central-city plants. Moreover, nonunion employees, low-wage workers, and newly hired workers . . . among which blacks are disproportionately represented, are most adversely affected by a recession-prone economy. They are not only the first to be dismissed, they are also those least likely to receive severance pay, unemployment benefits, or to be recalled on the job—in short, least likely to maintain ties to the world of work and means of economic self-sufficiency.[2]

The most fortunate and industrious inner-city residents found work in the growing service sector—in fast-food outlets or hospitals, as janitors, deliverymen, and the like—but at wages usually insufficient to support, or to encourage their starting, a family. Those in the inner city who could not get or would not take even low-level, low-paying jobs, including many who *wanted* to work and get ahead, but at decent jobs, found little else but idleness, anger, despair, nihilism, and crime, drug use and drug dealing.

If this was true for more and more adult males in 1964, as Moynihan had documented, it could only have been much worse for their male children five or ten years later, children with no strong working males at the head of their families and an ever-diminishing number of solid citizens in the ghetto community to set them a useful example.

Far fewer solid, hardworking, law-abiding citizens still live in the "black ghetto" than used to, though some have managed to remain. Increased affluence and better jobs elsewhere, distaste for life in a poverty area, the prevalence of crime, violence, prostitution, drug abuse—all have caused responsible and ambitious people to move to more desirable neighborhoods.

This has had reciprocally damaging effect on life in the inner city, eroding its tax base and speeding the closing of once-flourishing factories and stores. It has led to the departure of banking and credit facilities and to the decline of public services—the public schools and law enforcement in particular. And the exodus of the ghetto's most prominent symbols of stability, ambition, and moral fabric has left mostly drug dealers and street criminals to portray "success." Just as the poor have become poorer, poor urban areas have become much worse places to live.

"Inner city," "ghetto," and "underclass"* as a result have become common terms. Belatedly Americans have recognized that the cores of their cities, even of such formerly proud centers of industry as Detroit, are crime and drug-ridden jungles, where men and women are unemployed in large numbers, families are shattered, violence is rampant, despair has replaced hope, and children are flocking to the streets for lack of any more attractive or useful place to turn.

By the centennial year of 1976, about 25 million Americans still lived in poverty. Then things got rapidly worse; in 1983, 33 million—15.2 percent of the national population—were officially poor.[3]

Specifically, with the nation focused on the war in Vietnam in 1970, what later was commonly termed the underclass num-

---

*Dr. Poussaint deplores the word "underclass," calling it "a term devoid of hope." It has nevertheless become almost a necessary label for discussion and research, although, like any label, it tends to stick even after the contents of the package change.

bered only a little over 700,000, barely half a percent of the national population total. By 1980, however, a virtual explosion had taken place in the inner-city population: The urban under-class totaled nearly 2.5 million persons, or 1.37 percent of the U.S. population—an astonishing growth of *237 percent in a single decade.*

Such numbers, of course, depend on how the term "under-class" is defined. The calculations used here are by Ronald B. Mincy and Susan J. Weiner of the Urban Institute. They plau-sibly defined the underclass they were measuring not by areas or census tracts but as "people who have trouble entering and remaining in the labor force, and [who] derive much of their income from informal, illegal or irregular employment or from public assistance."[4]

By another measure, the number of persons living in poverty areas (census tracts where more than 20 percent of the population have incomes below the poverty level) in the nation's fifty largest cities increased by 20 percent in those same ten years, even though the same cities' *total* population declined by 5 percent.

At the end of the decade of the seventies more than half the poverty population was living in the ten largest of these cities: New York, Chicago, Los Angeles, Philadelphia, Detroit, Hous-ton, Baltimore, Dallas, Cleveland, and Indianapolis. Those cities alone were home to 40 percent of the urban black poor. Extreme poverty areas (census tracts where more than 40 percent live below the poverty line) had drastically expanded too; by 1980, 21 percent of all African-Americans in the ten largest cities lived in extreme poverty areas.

These major cities, once dominated by whites, seemed by 1980 to be overwhelmed by the underclass and its related problems: crime, violence, family breakdown, school dropouts, drugs, un-employment, dilapidated housing, teenage pregnancies. Most were precariously balanced politically between whites and mi-norities (with blacks and Hispanics, many of them poor, making up 43 percent of their populations). The decade had seen both an absolute and a relative increase in urban poverty, a continuing growth in the number of those living in high-poverty areas and the poorest sections of the ten cities, and a widening gap between the number of whites living in poverty and the increasing number of blacks suffering that fate.[5]

Mincy and Weiner found that the numerical expansion of the underclass slowed sharply in the 1980s, to only about 8 percent growth.[6] But the damage had been done; the underclass had become a blight on every large city in America and on the nation as a whole. The "pathologies" Moynihan had cited had radically altered the nation's view of African-Americans. And in terms of joblessness, crime, and despair, if not population, the situation in the ghetto was getting worse.

William Julius Wilson, an African-American sociologist at the University of Chicago, has cited three neighborhoods in that city—Oakland, Grand Boulevard, and Washington Park—as "stunning" examples of economic reversal:

> In 1950 there were 70 employed males for every 100 females ages 16 and over in these three communities. That was close to a city-wide figure of 74 working males per 100 females. By 1980, that figure had plummeted to 27/100 in Washington Park, 24/100 in Grand Boulevard, and 19 working males per 100 females in Oakland. We are talking here about a different kind of society.[7]

Indeed we are; such crushing losses of once-available jobs led not only to the obvious unemployment but to formerly productive, later discouraged black workers or their offspring dropping out of the labor market altogether, no longer even looking for a job (hence the Mincy-Weiner focus on "people who have trouble entering and remaining in the labor force").

As Charles Murray (long before he and Richard Herrnstein wrote *The Bell Curve*) pointed out in *Losing Ground,*[8] a controversial book about the underclass, these conditions hardly made idle young black males attractive marriage mates for young black females. Murray also contended that changes in welfare rules that had been intended to make life easier for welfare recipients actually made it more attractive for young women to choose welfare over marriage to men with dim prospects for anything but prison or the street corner. But the choice of welfare, he argued, led in turn to an increase in out-of-wedlock births,* an absence of strong male role models in the family, and a decline in fatherly discipline over children.

The problems of unlettered, unskilled, irresponsible ghetto mothers "supervising" children were graphically brought home to Jean Harris at Bedford Hills when a pregnant black woman complained to her that prison officials were not going to let her keep her baby in the prison nursery because she was known to have neglected her older children.

"Turn me down just 'cause I neglect my kids," the woman told Ms. Harris bitterly. "Neglect don't hurt. I never hit 'em, never broke anything. Just neglect don't hurt."[9]

Better-motivated or -educated young black females sometimes had a choice other than welfare. With women more welcome in the work force, they might choose jobs over marriage to black men unable to support a family. But this choice also led to out-of-wedlock births and single-parent families, sometimes, ironically, to children with an absent father and a working mother and *no* real family supervision. Yet the United States remains the only industrialized nation that does not offer families or working women a public child care system available to anyone needing it.

Charles Murray also found causative factors for inner-city decline in more permissive school and crime control policies. He charged too that guilt-ridden whites had decided that blacks with their history of oppression should not be held responsible for their actions, further weakening underclass fear of punishment and underclass will to engage in upward struggle.

Perhaps that attitude did develop among some of what he

---

*In fact, when antipoverty spending was at its highest, between 1964 and 1980, the birthrate among teenagers fell by a quarter. Unwed parenthood increased after 1980, when the value of the welfare package declined. Susan Mayer and Christopher Jencks, "War on Poverty: No Apologies, Please," *The New York Times* op-ed page, November 9, 1995.

termed the "intelligentsia and the policy makers," but the generality of the white population, as the backlash intensified, seemed more inclined to anger toward blacks. Else, how explain Richard Nixon's election and George Wallace's strong showing in 1968?

That year many white voters seemed to believe that the burning of cities, the black anger and nihilism the fires reflected, was a sort of "strange fruit" of the civil rights movement. But Murray's overall view, however disputed, is plausible. Visible as early as the Moynihan Report in 1965, destructive trends in the inner city *did* accelerate in the sixties and seventies. Well-intended social policy changes may have resulted in the weakening of responsibility and discipline among ghetto blacks.

Many other developments, however, obviously contributed—probably more—to the foul development of the inner city.

The Sheer Growth of Urban Populations

From 1960 to 1990 American cities were expanded by sixty-two million people, including the great migration of black share-croppers from the South into Chicago, Detroit, Baltimore, Washington, Los Angeles, and other urban centers, changing them forever. In the three decades ending in 1980 and spanning the ghetto explosion of the seventies, the black population of the thirty-three largest metropolitan areas increased by five million. Such growth profoundly strained urban educational, health, and law enforcement systems, and inevitably these stresses had their greatest impact on poor inner cities with less political power than affluent white areas.

Continuing Segregation in Housing

The fair housing legislation approved by Congress in 1968 is pitifully weak, providing no adequate enforcement powers. Housing discrimination and segregation therefore continue virtually unchecked, through mortgage loan discrimination in black, Hispanic, and changing areas, in the sometimes sly but often blatant "steering" practices of real estate agents,* and ow-ing to "white flight" from neighborhoods when blacks begin to move in.

Decades of theoretical integration have had no appreciable im-pact on housing segregation. In 1960, 35 percent of African-Americans lived in tracts that were 90 to 100 percent black; twenty years later that percentage had declined only marginally, to 31 percent, a proportion, moreover, that represented far more households than the 35 percent of 1960.

Housing patterns also are at the root of other forms of dis-advantage, obviously affecting job opportunities, for instance. If you can't live in a suburb, it's hard to get or hold a job there, and if you're forced to live in the inner city, few jobs are avail-able. Discriminatory mortgage funding, one of the mainstays of housing segregation, results in fewer black than white home-owners. That's a major reason why, in the mid-eighties, white families typically had eleven times the wealth of black families. Equity in a home is the main source of wealth for most people.

Racial Isolation

In the seventies and eighties, in both recession and inflation, poor blacks were hit particularly hard by rising unemployment, falling wages, and the decline in value of public assistance benefits. The result was soaring poverty. The director of the University of Chicago's Population Research Center has concluded:

> Virtually all of this increase in poverty was absorbed by a small number of isolated black neighborhoods. . . . The level of black poverty concentration skyrocketed. . . . Segregation was directly responsible for the emergence of this new, concentrated form of

*As late as February 1994 New York State's attorney general sued Places to Live, Inc., a Long Island referral service, for systematically misleading mi-norities about the availability of apartments and houses in white areas. That year about 90 percent of Long Island's African-American residents were concentrated in only 5 percent of its census tracts. Diana Jean Schemo, *The New York Times*, February 15, 1944, p. B1.

urban poverty [and] represents a primary structural factor behind the creation of the underclass.[10]

Continuing Segregation of Public Schools

Since the Supreme Court's *Milliken* decision of 1974 restricted
the ability of school districts to merge across metropolitan areas,
school desegregation has lagged, particularly in large northern
cities (as noted in Chapter Seven). The grudging, at best, desegregation of northern city schools is of vital importance. Fundamental differences exist, and can be demonstrated statistically,
between well-integrated or mostly white schools and the nearly
all-black schools of those northern cities. In schools in which
student bodies are predominantly minority, dropout levels are
higher, attendance records are worse, college entrance test taking
is down, precollegiate counseling is inadequate, and scholastic
achievement levels are dramatically lower.[11]

A Changing Economy

By the last third of this century seldom could unskilled workers
move up the economic scale by hard physical labor, the route to
the middle class taken by so many immigrants. Few black workers,
after years of discrimination in employment and education, had
had the opportunity to master technological or administrative skills.
Without them, manual laborers in modern times have been doomed
mostly to low-paying, low-status, sometimes dead-end jobs.

Asked from an audience of Harvard and Radcliffe students
why there was a 20 percent wage differential in favor of white
workers (an unsubstantiated figure) over black wage earners, the
sociologist Nathan Glazer replied that "the price of skill ha[d]
gone up" since the mid-eighties. Black workers were closing the
"skill gap," but "the price of skill" was rising faster than the gap
was closing.[12] This is a significant fact of economic—especially
African-American—life today.

Heightened Job Competition

Even low-skill, low-income jobs, however, have become harder
for blacks to find and keep. In the mid-sixties and since, women

entered the American labor market in great numbers, an over-due development. This influx was accompanied by the white baby boom cohort of the fifties, which came of working age in the seventies. Immigrants, legal and otherwise, often willing to take the lowest-status jobs, also provide stiff competition, particularly in the service sector one might have thought open to blacks dislodged from manufacturing jobs or those just entering the labor market.

Between 1970 and 1980, even as the overall economy was stalling, the national labor force was expanded by twenty-four million people, nearly twice the expansion of the sixties. This great growth occurred during a decade when black unemployment and the black underclass were rapidly expanding too. The connection seems obvious: More applicants—women, immigrants, baby boomers—meant that employers did not need or choose to hire as many black workers as they might once have. Young blacks seeking their first jobs, especially if they had not completed high school, were nearly always out of luck.[13]

Changing Values

In a society in demographic transformation, not just in the ghetto, attitudes have been undergoing wholesale change: on divorce, sexual fidelity, single parenthood, the military, the role of women, homosexuals, traditional family life.

Nor is it only in the inner city that the crime rate has risen; law enforcement, underfinanced and undermanned, seems overwhelmed everywhere. Vietnam-era draft evasion encouraged disregard for the law; widespread drug usage has ensnared many otherwise law-abiding persons. "Cops 'n' robbers" movies like *Dirty Harry* have popularized the idea that the only successful policeman is one who disregards the rules and the Constitution in order to exterminate those he considers bad guys.

The political system and government itself, notably in the 1994 election campaign, are widely protested, disdained, discredited—with Ronald Reagan, the Great Communicator, and Newt Gingrich, the new Speaker, having been among their most ardent critics. In 1995 the Oklahoma City bombing disclosed to aghast

Americans the existence of armed, organized opposition to even the idea of government.

The ghetto is not so isolated from changes in the larger society that its residents' behavior has developed in a sort of vacuum. Television and movies, after all, bring their dubious blessings to the inner city, as to other areas.

For all these reasons, by 1990, after a decade of mushrooming growth and another of near stability in population, the ghetto and the underclass loomed over American life like a thundercloud. Of the men in underclass areas, 59 percent were not in or seldom joined the labor force even briefly, more than twice the 23 percent level in a typical American neighborhood. The high school dropout rate in underclass areas was 38 percent against a U.S. average of 12 percent. Female-headed households were almost two thirds of all those in the underclass, though less than a quarter of all American households. The proportion of underclass families receiving public assistance was 300 percent greater than in the average U.S. census tract.[14]

Inevitably, and with much reason too, the black underclass—as it was usually considered—came to be seen by whites as the prime source of crime and violence in American cities and American life. Many, perhaps most, white Americans in the sixties had looked upon African-Americans as deserving descendants of oppressed slaves, brave marchers against Bull Connor's cattle prods. But as the underclass mushroomed, whites saw blacks instead as violent criminals, the rapists of the famous Central Park jogger, the muggers lurking in the alley, the threatening presence that made crime a dreaded urban commonplace.

Of all the misfortunes, misunderstandings, and misconceptions that shaped the backlash, that white perception of uncontrollable black crime may have been the most damaging to African-Americans.

10 Throwing Away the Key

The larger and tougher prisons and jails of the
United States give the impression of institutions
for segregating the young black and Hispanic
male underclass from society.

Norval Morris

On November 13, 1993, to an African-American congregation in Memphis and from Martin Luther King's last pul-
pit, President Clinton spoke with an emotionalism reported to
have surprised his White House staff. The president declared
that Dr. King, if alive today, might say:

> I did not live and die to see the American family destroyed. I
> did not live and die to see 13-year-old boys get automatic weap-
> ons and gun down 9-year-olds just for the kick of it. I did not
> live and die to see young people destroy their own lives with
> drugs and then build fortunes destroying the lives of others. . . .
> I fought for freedom . . . but not for the freedom of people to
> kill each other with reckless abandonment, and not for the free-
> dom of children to have children and the fathers of the children
> to walk away from them . . . as if they don't amount to any-
> thing.[1]

Clinton was not alone among whites *or* blacks in fearing that black violence was endangering the "fabric of our society." But the faith he expressed in his preacherly peroration is not so widely shared: "We will turn this around. We will give these children a future. We will take away their guns and give them books. We will take away their despair and give them hope. We will rebuild the families and the neighborhoods and the communities."

Reaching this goal, the president said, was "our moral duty," and he insisted that it could and would be done "somehow, by God's grace." But he also told the Memphis congregation that the fabric of society could not be mended "until people *who are willing to work have work*," that crime and violence were consequences of "the breakdown of the family, the community, and *the disappearance of jobs*," and that therefore "we [must] provide the structure, the values, the discipline, and the reward *that work gives*" (emphasis added).

This thrice-repeated prescription disclosed Clinton's understanding that the disappearance of jobs is the most pressing problem of the ghetto. But God's grace is not noted, unfortunately, for bringing down the unemployment rate, and if the lack of jobs is as vital a part of the underclass problem as Clinton declared, programs to create jobs for those trapped in the ghetto might plausibly be considered necessary.

The president suggested no such programs. In a familiar American pattern he made no more than a moral appeal to blacks—not to whites or to the society they dominate—to do and be better, to rise above difficulties mostly imposed upon the ghetto by socioeconomic conditions in a nation controlled by whites. About those conditions he was silent too.

Only the black community, moreover, was exhorted by the president "to reach deep inside to the values, the spirit, the soul, and the truth of human nature." Only African-Americans, he seemed to be saying, should repair the basic fabric of a society they did not create, do not control, and from which the children he cited remain cruelly excluded.

A quarter century ago Martin Luther King actually did counsel "desperate, rejected and angry young men" to eschew violence. Their response, in those years of extreme American violence in Vietnam, transformed him:

> They asked if our own nation wasn't using massive doses of violence to solve its problems, to bring about the changes it wanted. Their questions hit home, and I knew that I could never again raise my voice against the violence of the oppressed in the ghettos without having first spoken clearly to the greatest purveyor of violence in the world today—my own government.[2]

The war in Vietnam of course is ended. So is the Cold War. But the United States of Bill Clinton remains, as King characterized the America of three decades ago, "a nation that continues year after year to spend more money on military offense" than on improving economic opportunity. A nation following such policies, King believed in 1967, "is approaching spiritual death."

Had he actually been in Memphis in 1993, that's what he might still have said.

Most whites probably would be surprised to know that the black proportion of the underclass population actually declined, if only slightly, from 66 percent in 1970 to 58 percent in 1990 and that the white percentage grew, in the same years, from 21 to 27.[3] Still, however, to legions of white and more fortunate Americans, the term "underclass" almost automatically means poor blacks, just as the word "ghetto" means a poor, drug-ridden, crime-producing *black* neighborhood.

White fear of crime is directed primarily at the underclass, at the ghetto; white fear of crime therefore has become fear of African-Americans. That fear, however exaggerated, is a salient fact of life in the American city today, breeding the suspicion and animosity from which it is only a short jump to hatred.

City people living with three locks on their doors, afraid to walk the dog after dark, and seeing every night on TV (a major influence) the evidence of violent crime, often with an African-American suspect either in custody or being sought, are not inclined to be analytical or judicious about black crime. Never mind that most of it occurs in the generally distant, deprived streets of underclass neighborhoods and that other blacks are often the victims. The contemporary white attitude toward all African-Americans is strongly conditioned by the white perception of the lawless behavior of what whites think of as the black underclass.

What modern urban-dwelling white has not had the experience of walking alone down a city block, seeing a black male approaching, and feeling a sudden fear, perhaps even crossing the street to avoid a head-on meeting? Blacks are all too familiar with this reaction, a *white* reaction. Brent Staples, an African-American who is now a member of the editorial board of *The New York Times*, has recalled the first time he noticed it, years ago on Fifty-seventh Street in Chicago:

> [T]here she was, a few yards ahead of me, dressed in business clothes and carrying a brief case. She looked back at me once, then again, and picked up her pace. She looked back again and started to run. . . . I'd been a fool. I'd been grinning good evening at people who were frightened to death of me. I did violence to them just by being.

Once alerted to this phenomenon, Staples "became expert in the language of fear": "People who were carrying on conversations went mute and stared straight ahead, as though avoiding my eyes would save them. This reminded me of the old wives' tale that rabid dogs didn't bite if you avoided their eyes."

In a larger sense than Staples may have intended, that's not a bad metaphor for the white attitude toward the inner city: Don't look at it, don't notice, don't do anything about it, and maybe it won't bite. But even Brent Staples, for a while, took a perverse pleasure in frightening whites he met on the street at night. That, his memoir makes clear, was only a means of concealing from himself, or compensating for, the hurt, humiliation, and anger of such an everyday occurrence for male African-Americans.[4]

John Hope Franklin's well-educated son, a professional employed at the Smithsonian Institution in Washington, often has suffered a different but equally humiliating experience. In that city it's not unusual to see the locked door of a store displaying a sign saying *Ring for Entrance*—a symbol of the fear pervading cities these days, Washington more than most. Franklin has several times seen white store employees, hearing his ring, refuse to open the door, not so much to deny entrance to *him* as to *any* African-American.[5]

White police officers are among the most egregious offenders in assuming that blackness equals criminality. On May 1, 1995, two white transit police officers in New York grabbed the elbows of a black man leaving a train at Grand Central Station, stood him against a wall, took his briefcase, ordered him to raise his arms, and frisked him as commuters streamed by in the morning rush hour.

The officers found nothing because the man was Earl G. Graves, Jr., a senior vice president for *Black Enterprise* magazine. The police were acting on a tip to look out for a black man with an athletic build, about five feet ten inches tall, with a mustache, and carrying a gun. Graves has a former basketball player's physique, but he is six feet four and has no mustache. He is black, however, and for that reason alone, he had several times before been accosted and questioned by white policemen.[6]

Whites can only respond to such mistakes by asking how were they to know that the approaching black stranger was a lawyer or an editorial writer and a decent citizen, not a mugger. But however rationalized or seemingly justified in modern urban life, that reaction—lumping together *everybody* of a certain color in a degrading stereotype, depriving them all of individuality—is humiliating to those who suffer it. And the fear at the root of this frequent white reaction is too near panic to be defended.

With fear of crime prevailing to a degree impossible for politicians to ignore—though, ironically, many have stimulated the fear themselves, with sensationalized speeches about crime and violence—get-tough crime laws have flourished, long mandatory minimum prison sentences have been imposed, sometimes even on minor drug offenders, and white housing developments just short of armed fortresses have sprung up. Curfews on teenagers are being seriously discussed, notably in Florida, and by 1994 two dozen cities had adopted them.

Even liberals like former Governor Mario Cuomo of New York, as well as the so-called new Democrat Bill Clinton, called for "three strikes and you're out" laws, lifetime sentences without possibility of parole for persons convicted of third felonies. A three-strike provision was included in Clinton's crime bill, passed in 1994, not least because polls showed that about 80 percent of Americans favored this supposedly hard-nosed tactic.*

A *Wall Street Journal*–NBC poll in May 1994 found that by two to one Americans favored tougher law enforcement rather than increased economic opportunity as the most effective way to reduce crime. Eight in ten believed that putting a hundred thousand more police officers on the street would help. And by 78 to 12 percent they favored long prison terms for violent offenders, even if as a result nonviolent criminals had to go free to make cells available.

Because of perceived ghetto behavior, especially crime and violence but also welfare abuses, the "crack" cocaine epidemic, and out-of-wedlock births, politicians note a new public reluctance, highly visible in the 1994 elections and well reflected in the rhetoric of Newt Gingrich, to support social programs. Again, the demagogic speeches of politicians and others have encouraged this resistance.

As President Clinton has lamented, "People are scared. It is very difficult for me to give a speech on the global economy and all my retraining and investment ideas when people don't even think their kids can go to school safely. It is a very basic thing. It unites people across deep divides."[7]

*See footnote, p. 40.

That concern perhaps explains why Clinton opted for what was primarily a punitive crime bill. Philip Heymann, Clinton's first deputy attorney general, resigned in February 1994, among other reasons because he opposed many of the bill's provisions: "three strikes," new prisons, mandatory minimum sentences for minor drug offenders—all politically popular proposals that Heymann and numerous criminologists believed would have little effect on crime. If ways could be devised for the $22.3 billion then proposed for such headline-grabbing purposes to be spent on the provision of jobs for unemployed persons in the inner city, many crimes might be prevented rather than a few being punished.[8]

Reason, however, seldom quiets fear and anger. A white person mugged by a black (a frequent event) or a white who believes him- or herself menaced by a black (more frequent) or a white outraged by welfare costs and out-of-wedlock births (probably even more frequent) typically becomes more resistant to efforts to improve the economic and social lot of the poor because they inevitably include the feared African-Americans.

The paradox seems not to be apparent to those who prefer instead to "lock 'em up and throw away the key" or to put black women receiving welfare to work, without much regard for what will become of their children.

The white perception of African-American males as criminals is inaccurate and unfair, and it's partially self-stimulating, largely because of public support for get-tough law enforcement and public disdain for social programs. Perceiving themselves as opposing crime, citizens holding these attitudes actually may be making crime more prevalent, thus heightening their fear of crime and violence.

On a single day in Washington in 1991, of all black males aged eighteen to thirty-five in the District of Columbia, *42 percent* were in some manner in collision with the criminal justice system: 15 percent in prison; 21 percent on probation; 6 percent awaiting trial or sought by the police.

At about the same time in nearby Baltimore, *56 percent* of eighteen- to thirty-five-year-old black males were incarcerated, on probation or parole, awaiting trial, or being sought for arrest. In the United States as a whole the differential rate of imprisonment for blacks and whites per hundred thousand of population has risen to about *7.5 to 1*. This means that more than seven times as many blacks as whites, proportional to population, will be in American jails or prisons at any given time.

In 1995, the Sentencing Project of Washington reported that one in three black males in the age group 20 to 29 was under some form of criminal justice supervision on any given day. That's 827,440 persons, an increase from one in four just five years ago.

Yet African-Americans are only about 12 percent of the population, and numerous studies show that middle-class African-Americans (perhaps 40 percent of the 12 percent) are no more criminal or violent than their white contemporaries. Popular belief notwithstanding, crime and delinquency rates for whites and blacks in similar socioeconomic circumstances *are virtually indistinguishable.*[9]

Obviously, then, it's disadvantaged inner-city underclass blacks, not African-Americans in general, who commit crimes and go to prison at grossly higher rates than whites. It's also ghetto blacks, being nearer at hand and not usually so well defended either by the law or by their housing arrangements, who are most often the victims of underclass criminals. Homicide, for instance, has become the principal cause of death among young black males.

These facts do little to ease the fearful mood gripping the nation, a mood owing mostly to underclass behavior (not that of African-Americans generally) and shared by both races but most loudly expressed by whites. That's why states, localities, and the federal government are feverishly but usually ineffectively trying to get tough on crime. Instead of putting idle people to work or offering other forms of assistance, they're following the failed and failing policy of "lock 'em up and throw away the key," a crackdown on the black underclass that may respond to the *fear* of crime, though probably stimulating it too, but does little about the *fact* of crime.

The land of the free and the home of the brave now puts more of its citizens in prison—373 per 100,000 of its population—than any other nation, except what used to be the Soviet Union and including South Africa at the height of its apartheid policy.

Thirteen states now have smaller populations than that of state and federal prisons and jails: 1,012,851 persons in prisons on June 30, 1994, and 445,000 in local jails the last time they were counted, in 1992. In the first six months of 1994 the U.S. prison population grew by nearly 40,000 inmates, the equivalent of building and filling about fifteen hundred new prisons a week.[10]

Combine these shocking facts with the highly disproportionate incarceration of African-Americans—more than seven times as many as whites, out of only 12 percent of the population—and it's no wonder that the criminologist Norval Morris can say, "The larger and tougher prisons and jails of the United States ... give the impression of institutions for segregating the young black and Hispanic male underclass from society."[11]

For all practical purposes, that is exactly what they are. The Sentencing Project of Washington estimates that the 583,000 African-American males behind bars outnumber those enrolled in higher education, about 537,000. And if many white and perhaps some black Americans had their way, more of the "young black and Hispanic male underclass" would be behind bars, "segregated from society" (but only temporarily, since most inevitably will return someday to the streets).

Public opinion and political action, moreover, are making the already tough world of the American prison tougher yet. Alabama and Arizona have renewed use of the chain gang. In Mississippi inmates now must wear striped uniforms displaying the word "convict." At least ten states are considering caning as a disciplinary measure for inmates. Television, weight lifting, and other forms of prison recreation are under attack everywhere and have been discontinued in some prisons. A median of only

9 percent of state prison inmates are usefully employed in prison industries, although the figure rises as high as 30 percent in some states. New Jersey and Connecticut are now charging prison inmates for some medical services and medications.

These stick-wielding measures ignore what James Stabile, communications director for New Jersey's Department of Corrections, calls "the need to have some carrots in a prison setting where you are dealing with people doing long terms with mandatory minimums." It's people who "have never been in a prison" or "seen how tough it is" inside, he says, who call for more get-tough steps.

Nevertheless, the Supreme Court, aware as always of election returns, has made it harder for inmates to bring lawsuits to vindicate what they assert as a constitutional right. Chief Justice William Rehnquist's opinion for a five-to-four majority declared that such suits would be limited in future to those appealing against an "atypical and significant hardship." In practice that will give prison administrators "greater flexibility" in what Rehnquist called "the fine-tuning of the ordinary incidents of prison life."*

"Getting tough" through imprisonment is what Americans have chosen, in ignorance, fear, mistake, or malice, to do about the children of the ghetto, undoubtedly the most threatening but also the neediest sources of violence and crime in contemporary American life. And a destructive side effect of an aggressive imprisonment policy is that it sustains many African-Americans' strong—and by no means irrational—sense that the criminal justice system is biased against their race.

Shortly before the first Rodney King trial in Los Angeles, an associate professor of government at Harvard named Katherine Tate placed a telephone call to her mother, who lives in the South. The daughter, the author of a book on African-American voting trends,[12] was sure the white police officers who had beaten King would be convicted. Their actions had been videotaped and

---

*Rehnquist was joined in the majority, as usual, by Justices O'Connor, Scalia, Kennedy, and Thomas.

widely televised, and she thought their guilt could not be doubted.

Tate therefore was surprised to hear her mother, whom she described as a rather traditional African-American who had never been an activist, express the quiet conviction that the white officers would be acquitted. Her mother, Ms. Tate concluded, had a "visceral feeling" that black people never get justice in white America, a "visceral feeling" that the end of segregation in the South had failed to erase from many African-American psyches.

The first King verdict—not guilty—can only have deepened that "visceral feeling." Katherine Tate herself asked me in tones of hurt and bewilderment: "Why are white people like they are?"[13]

Her mother had good reason to doubt the outcome of the King case because antiblack bias is everywhere in the criminal justice system. In New York State young African-Americans are *twenty-three times* more likely to be imprisoned than white men. Three times more young whites are on probation than are in New York prisons, but for blacks the opposite is true.

The death penalty is notorious for racial bias, and not just in the Deep South. Under the 1988 drug kingpin law, the Justice Department was empowered to seek death for drug-related murders by big narcotics operators and their associates. At the time of writing, execution had been sought for forty-two such defendants, thirty-seven of them African-Americans. *But three fourths of all drug-trafficking defendants are white.* Nor was this a hangover from the Reagan and Bush administrations; in 1993 Bill Clinton's attorney general, Janet Reno, sought ten death penalties under the 1988 law, and all ten defendants were black.

Differing federal penalties for possession and use of powdered cocaine and crack cocaine show the same pattern of racial bias—whether or not so intended. A nonviolent first offender convicted in federal court of possessing five grams of crack receives a mandatory minimum sentence of five years in prison. Possession of five grams of powdered cocaine, on the other hand, is only a misdemeanor, punishable at worst by a year in prison.

Crack defendants, however, are much more likely to be black, because crack is cheaper and easily available in underclass neighborhoods. Only about 4 percent of crack defendants are white, although in 1993 a national survey found that 46 percent of crack smokers were white. And since federal law treats a gram of crack as the equivalent of one hundred grams of powdered cocaine, minor (mostly black) street pedlars of crack can and do get the long, harsh sentences mandated for major (often white) dealers in powdered cocaine.[14]

As a result of the Los Angeles riots of 1992, it took two trials before two of the four police officers videotaped beating Rodney King were sentenced to thirty months in prison. But a little later a white judge sentenced Damian Williams, an African-American, to the maximum prison term of ten years for the brutal beating of three men, one a white truck driver, during the riots. At sentencing Judge John J. Ouderkirk told Williams that it was "intolerable in this society to attack and maim people because of their race."[15]

After the beating of Rodney King, which seemed "intolerable" to many Americans, white and black, and the light sentencing of only half the white men—policemen at that—who had manhandled him, Judge Ouderkirk's ten-year sentence against a black civilian for a similar offense, as well as his ringing lecture, angered African-Americans. The Reverend Cecil Murray of the First AME Church of Los Angeles observed that "contextually, this says to blacks that the pattern of history continues." And Roy Evans, who heads a work furlough program for juvenile offenders, called Williams's sentence "an excellent example of the kind of dual justice we have in Southern California, one for blacks and one for whites."

This black perception of dual systems of justice may well have been a major factor in late 1995 in the acquittal of the football star and movie actor O. J. Simpson, in his celebrated trial on charges of murdering his former wife Nicole and her friend Ronald Goldman. Most whites, every indicator showed, believed

Simpson had been proved guilty by the evidence. A jury with seven black members nevertheless found him not guilty.

One reason appeared to have been that the jury believed some evidence provided by the Los Angeles Police Department had been faked or planted, particularly by Detective Mark Fuhrman, and should have been inadmissible. Testimony in the trial showed Fuhrman to hold virulent racist views, and blacks— particularly residents of Los Angeles—almost universally consider the LAPD racist and corrupt.

Many blacks celebrated Simpson's acquittal, perhaps because in some cases they saw it as a racial victory over an antiblack justice system. The contrast between this view and the white expectation of a guilty verdict appears to have shocked the white community, at least temporarily, into realization of the nation's deep-seated racial division.

For the first six months of 1995 an apparently significant drop in murder rates from the same period in 1994 was reported in some of the nation's largest cities: from 478 homicides to 388 in Chicago, for example, 238 to 196 in New Orleans, 826 to 563 in New York, and 203 to 138 in Houston. Decreases of varying numbers also were observed in Atlanta, Boston, Los Angeles, Philadelphia, St. Louis, even Detroit and Washington, D.C.

Police and other officials were quick to claim that get-tough law enforcement was showing results. But it didn't in Dallas, Phoenix, Minneapolis, or Gary, Indiana, where the murder rates went up. The national rate—9.9 homicides per 100,000 persons in 1993, the last full year for which figures are available—is about the same as it was sixty years ago, in 1933: 10 per 100,000.

Besides, persons aged fourteen to seventeen were killing people at the rate of *nearly 19 per 100,000* in 1993, and the teenage population is expected by the Census Bureau to increase by 15 percent in the next decade. So the murder rate, which historically tends to rise and fall for reasons not always clear, may well rise again by the end of the century or sooner.[16]

More people in prison means fewer people free to commit crimes, including murder—in the short run perhaps, but as all those current inmates return to the streets in the future, that may not hold true. Even that much is being achieved, if it is, at horrendous cost, social as well as economic. And though some prisons are necessary for separating the most dangerous and violent criminals (if they can be identified) from society, for the larger purpose of reducing crime, imprisonment doesn't work as well as advertised. And despite the striking increase in the American prison population in recent decades—in California, the bellwether state, to 382 persons per 100,000, a total of 124,813[17]—actual crime has not been much diminished (that apparent decline in murder rates, which may not be long-lasting, notwithstanding).

If socioeconomic conditions in the ghetto remain the same or get worse, as they have, then for every young criminal snatched from the inner city and lodged in prison, another, or more than one—bred by the same squalid conditions of idleness and despair—will take his place. The process is not dissimilar to college juniors replacing a graduating class, and the comparison is not fanciful because going to prison is more expectable in the ghetto than is going to college.

Besides, imprisonment costs too much for what it accomplishes. Keeping more than a million people in custody, as the United States currently does, costs states, localities, and the federal government about sixteen billion dollars a year. Since about 43 percent of the prison population is black and since most black inmmates are from the inner city, it's reasonable to estimate that locking up underclass blacks alone costs perhaps six or seven billion dollars a year.

If the U.S. rate of imprisonment should keep growing at the pace of July–December 1989—7.3 percent—Americans soon will be adding ninety thousand inmates a year to the prison population (forty thousand were added in the first half of 1994), nearly half of them African-Americans at present ratios. That would demand 250 new cells, at a cost of $12.5 million, *per day*.[18]

Sky-high and rising imprisonment rates, moreover, are not caused by equally sky-high and rising crime rates, as generally supposed by frightened city dwellers and the politicians who try to placate them. In fact, the incidence of serious crimes *declined* somewhat in the period 1980-85, while an increase in the 1985-92 period was not enough to boost the rate back to its high 1980 level. Uniform crime reports from law enforcement agencies and victim surveys agree on these trends.

Therefore imprisonment has increased, the criminologist Norval Morris asserts, not because more crimes were committed but because of public, police, prosecution, and judicial get-tough attitudes. In Morris's judgment, the get-tough approach also was responsible for doubling the number of women in prison, from 3 to 6 percent of the total prison population, in the last decade. There's been no commensurate rise in crime by females.*

Nor is crime in the United States, underclass or no underclass, out of all proportion to crime in other countries. Despite popular belief, scare headlines, and sensational television shows, crime rates here, including the rate of assaults, are generally comparable to those in Western Europe, Canada, and Australia, with two substantial exceptions:

- The possession and sale of prohibited drugs, which are far more common in the United States
- The *consequences* of assaults, which tend more often here to result in death or serious injury

The obvious reason for the second is the easy availability of guns, even automatic weapons, to inner-city and other criminals.[19] It could also be argued plausibly that the acceptance of violence—for instance, guns supposedly for the self-defense of law-abiding citizens—in a historically violent culture has much to do with high rates of injury and death.

That acceptance, of course, is one reason for the ease with which guns can be acquired in America, legally or otherwise, and therefore for the Children's Defense Fund calculation that nearly fifty thousand American children and teenagers were

*Predictably, according to the Sentencing Project, African-American women have suffered a greater increase in their rate of criminal justice control—up 78 percent from 1989 to 1994—than any other population group.

killed by firearms—twenty-four thousand in homicides—between 1979 and 1991.

A Justice Department survey of ten inner-city high schools in 1993 found that 22 percent of male pupils reported owning a gun; 12 percent of these males said they routinely carried a gun. Nearly 70 percent of all pupils reported guns present in their homes. The same report found that guns of all varieties, including military rifles, were readily available in areas near the schools surveyed.

Nothing seems to cool Americans' passion for guns, and not just in the ghetto or among criminals. Even a wave of public revulsion *against* guns, following Colin Ferguson's shooting spree on a Long Island Rail Road train in 1993, resulting in six dead and many more wounded, stimulated handgun sales (which had been booming anyway). Gun dealers across the nation reported that ordinary citizens were hurrying to buy guns for self-protection (as they thought) before government, heeding the outcry against Ferguson's and others' atrocities, might ban or restrict handgun sales or ownership.[20]

Such a ban, of course, is most unlikely, given the state of public opinion on the subject and widespread misunderstanding of the Fourth Amendment. The Bureau of Alcohol, Tobacco, and Firearms, estimates that already there are about 210 million guns of all types in the United States—nearly one for every American—or twice as many as fifty years ago. Not many politicians are going to vote restrictions with teeth on that many people—those who must possess these guns.*

For all its cost and even with 373 out of every 100,000 Americans behind bars, moreover, imprisonment doesn't protect society very well. Owing to overburdened and underfinanced law enforcement, only about 20 percent of crimes result in an arrest,

---

*The possibility arose in the summer of 1995 that the Oklahoma City bombing might have been perpetrated by militants who feared gun control and sought revenge against ATF and FBI agents for their assault on the Branch Davidian cult in Waco, Texas, in 1993. If that proves true, it might conceivably lessen the ardor of anti–gun control but law-abiding forces in America.

not all of these lead to convictions, and even fewer produce prison terms for an offender. In early 1994 *The Boston Globe* reported that more than 1,000 people charged with felonies in Suffolk County, Massachusetts, had not appeared for trial. And whatever deterrent effects prisons may have, they clearly have not stopped the development of young criminals to take the places of those unlucky or inept enough to serve time.

All inmates, moreover, can't be kept behind bars forever. Sooner or later, even where three-strike laws may come into force, most inmates (an estimated 95 percent) will be returned to the community (if for no other reason than the necessity otherwise to build more and more costly prison cells). As things already are in most jurisdictions, prisons are so expensive to build and operate and so overcrowded that many inmates serve perhaps only a third of their sentences.

And whom are we putting in prison? Serial killers? Vicious rapists? Some, perhaps, but a lot more minor narcotics violators. In 1980 only 19 of every 1,000 persons arrested for such offenses went to prison; by 1992, again owing to fear-induced get-tough policies, a fivefold increase in imprisonment put 104 of every 1,000 arrested for a drug offense behind bars. Drug offenders are the largest growth group in American prisons. Their numbers grew about 510 percent, from an estimated 57,975 in 1983 to 353,564 in 1993.

Sometimes it's the wastage of a frightened society that does time. In New York State at least two thirds of blacks incarcerated are high school dropouts. Nationally, the Justice Department reports, 70 percent of crimes have something to do with drugs; many others were the result of alcohol consumption. Of the women imprisoned at Bedford Hills, Jean Harris observed in her speech at Dana College that "one in five is HIV positive. More and more come in with TB and congenital syphilis.... They have herpes, high blood pressure, cervical cancer, seizures, ugly untreated scars from where they've been slashed with knives, and teeth that have never seen a dentist."

A recent national survey of prison women indicated that half of them had run away from home as youths, about a quarter had attempted suicide, many had serious drug problems, half were victims of physical abuse, and 36 percent of sexual abuse. These are the kind of people we're sending to prison in the national panic over crime—*and* the people we return to the streets, often in even worse shape physically, mentally, and spiritually than when they went behind bars.

Given the lawlessness, violence, and inhumanity of most prisons—nowhere are law enforcement officers less able to protect the general population under their charge from predators—and the general absence of useful job training, health, and rehabilitative programs for inmates (not to mention minor offenders' years of forced association with career criminals and sociopaths), the released inmate often goes back to the streets a more embittered, hopeless, self-hating, economically incompetent, and criminally inclined person (perhaps less healthy and newly drug-addicted) than he or she was when incarcerated. If he or she returns to the same old hopeless conditions, as most do, his or her return to prison for another crime is all but guaranteed.

In 1994 John Whitley, the warden at Angola, Louisiana's prison farm—certainly no "country club" even though reformed from its former infamy—awarded diplomas to fifty-seven inmates who had completed paralegal and computer courses while doing their time. In his "commencement address," Whitley warned that this might be the last such "graduating class" from Angola. Why? Because in the new federal crime bill pushed by Bill Clinton, funding for postsecondary education for prisoners was eliminated, even though statistics show that college courses for inmates reduce recidivism rates from as high as 70 percent to as low as 15 to 30 percent.

Similarly, New York State now has prohibited its prison inmates from receiving subsidies to take college courses while behind bars. That ended a twenty-year program by 23 two- and four-year colleges in forty-five New York prisons. In most of those years about thirty-five hundred inmates had received such subsidies and about nine hundred were awarded degrees. Recently the state had been granting about five million dollars in educational subsidies to inmates from its six-hundred-million-dollar Tuition Assistance Program. About 1 percent of TAP recipients were in prison; the rest were the children of the state's taxpayers.

New York's Correctional Services Department followed the activities of 356 inmates who took degrees with TAP subsidies in 1987 and were released by 1990. They compiled a 26.4 percent rate of return to prison, compared with *48 percent* of the general prison population released in the same period.

Reducing educational opportunities for inmates is "getting tough"; it's also a self-defeating approach to crime prevention and reduction. As Robert Ferrara, a convicted murderer who received a B.A. at Sing Sing in 1995, one of the last inmates who will do so, put it, "This has been the single most important thing I've ever done in my whole life. This should have been the last thing they took away from us. If anything in the world is going to help men grow and change, it's education."[21]

John Whitley's address to the graduates at Angola included a devastating indictment of get-tough schemes like more and harsher prisons, longer sentences, more death penalties, and three-strike laws. "Let's look at a state that has tried them for the past 20 years," he said, pointing out that Louisiana now has twelve prisons instead of three, has lengthened sentences until it has the "harshest penalties in the nation," has executed twenty-one people since 1983, and for more than fifteen years has had laws "that for all practical purposes mean one strike and you're out."

Is Louisiana, as a result, measurably safer? "Only a few months ago," Whitley said (in 1994), "Louisiana was declared the most dangerous [state] in the nation in which to live."[22]

11 Middle-Class Blues

The odds are against any of you making it.

Earvin "Magic" Johnson
(to black high school students)

Not long before Vernon Jordan, the prosperous African-American lawyer who once headed the Urban League, became cochairman of President-elect Bill Clinton's transition committee in 1992, he went to see *Boyz N the Hood*, a scathing film about life in the black youth gangs of Los Angeles in the nineties.

Jordan saw in the movie "a lot of things I don't know about"—a scarred and scary urban landscape and a life very different from those he had known growing up fifty years ago in legally segregated Atlanta.

The black middle class, as he knew it then, and the black poor, he told me in tones of faint bewilderment, used to live closely together. Now it seemed to him that perhaps "the civil rights movement has been so successful that they've been allowed to separate."[1]

"Induced" might be a better word, and it's not so clear that separation is success.

*　*　*

In his Memphis speech, as he imagined what Martin Luther King might say were he to return to life, President Clinton, though he focused on crime, said King would approve of the new black middle class: "[You] did a good job creating a black middle class of people who really are doing well, and the middle class is growing more among African-Americans than among non-African-Americans. . . . You did a good job in opening opportunity."

"At least for *some* African-Americans," Clinton or King might have added. Earlier that year Henry Louis Gates, the director of the Harvard black studies program, gave me the "horseback" estimate that of today's African-American population, about 40 percent were in the middle class, 30 percent were in the underclass, and the rest were somewhere in between, many moving toward one of the other groups.*

William Julius Wilson also cites a larger than supposed black middle class. Of the twenty-nine million African-Americans, he estimates that "about 20 percent are in the professional middle class [lawyers, doctors, etc.] with another 15 percent in non credentialed white collar positions," a total of 35 percent in something like middle class or better status.[2]

Many whites would be surprised by Clinton's statement at Memphis that "the middle class is growing more among African-Americans" than among whites. But it is.[†] In 1960 a mere 20 percent of African-Americans could be defined by income as middle class (having incomes, that is, two to five times the poverty level). By the early seventies that figure had nearly doubled, to 38 percent—close to Gates's estimate and well beyond most white perceptions.

The increase slowed sharply thereafter (just as the growth of the underclass tapered off in the eighties), but still, by 1987–88,

---

*Gates's estimates were not statistically documented, but he believed they gave a generally accurate picture of the black community.
†The black middle class was smaller to begin with, of course, and many whites have moved still farther up the income ladder from the middle into the "affluent" class.

43 percent of African-Americans had incomes at least twice the poverty level.[3] And they could take advantage of their relative economic prosperity in a classic American way: They could and did move to a better—but only sometimes white—neighborhood.

The percentage of blacks living in neighborhoods 90 to 100 percent black fell from 35 in 1960 to 31 in 1980, but the latter proportion, owing to population growth, represented a larger number of households. At the other end of the segregation spectrum the number of black households in areas less than 20 percent black rose from 13 to 17 percent in the same period.[4]

This change by no means achieved "housing integration," and a high degree of residential segregation remains today (see Chapter Nine). But it was a substantial change for those who could move to more affluent streets than those of the ghetto. That became possible for economically successful African-Americans because of civil rights gains generally, more specifically owing to local, state, ultimately federal fair housing regulations, despite some obvious weaknesses, and particularly because of a Supreme Court decision banning racially restrictive covenants in leases and deeds.

This new mobility tends to bear out Vernon Jordan's observation that the civil rights movement has put distance between the black poor and the black middle class. In many ways, however, that's an unfortunate distance and a mixed blessing, as William Julius Wilson has observed: "Thirty years ago there was much greater class integration in black communities. Though they may have lived on different streets, blacks of all classes lived in the same neighborhood. Their kids went to the same schools and played in the same parks. Thus, their neighborhoods at that time were more stable."[5]

That sounds not unlike the black community in Atlanta when Vernon Jordan grew up there. In the inner city left behind by newly mobile middle-class blacks in recent decades, that stability deteriorated rapidly. Female-headed households, jobless men, drug addicts and alcoholics, the drug trade, and a criminal element became dominant. As achieving and law-abiding male breadwinners, those who had been the black community's standard setters, its pillars of stability, discipline, family, and societal values, moved their families elsewhere, they left the inner city poorer, more lawless and violent.

The irony was acute. Despite the difficulties and disappointments of desegregation, despite continuing prejudice and discrimination, numerous African-Americans had made economic progress that compared well with or bettered that of whites moving up from poorer status into the middle class. But one terrible result was the degradation of the ghetto, the communities they had left behind.

Another was that their substantial accomplishments were largely overlooked by whites who were more powerfully and emotionally impressed by the crime and violence newly prevalent in those communities, the inner city. The growth of the black middle class was largely lost to view in the lurid new visibility of the underclass remaining in the ghetto.

Vernon Jordan is not only a presidential confidant, a powerful player in Democratic party politics, but one of the most successful American lawyers, with a seat on eleven corporate boards paying him more than half a million dollars a year. Few careers better illustrate what Charles Hamilton of Columbia University, the author of *Black Power* and Adam Clayton Powell's biography, cites as a goal of the civil rights movement: "to maximize opportunities."

Shirley Chisholm, the first black woman presidential candidate, agrees: "The idea in this country for most people is to feel that they are part of the wonderful American dream that everybody talks about. So why should Vernon Jordan be any different from any white who was also poor? And if he can eat lobsters and . . . enjoy the good life, why not?"[6]

Nevertheless, though most African-Americans are impressed and some are gratified by achievements like Jordan's, many question what price has to be paid for them and what effect, if any, they will have on the black community generally.

What have Jordan's prominence and his ties to President Clinton done for other blacks, those at the lowest economic level in particular? How will the prosperity of successful middle-class blacks, well removed from the ghetto, help isolated young people in the ghetto develop the habits and values needed for getting and keeping mainstream jobs?

Those are difficult questions. In personal terms, is a newly affluent African-American as entitled to enjoy his or her prosperity as anyone else and as he or she might choose? Or as an African-American, with a share in the race's history and tribulations, does he or she have an obligation to that race transcending any white's responsibility to other whites? If the latter, how can that obligation be met?

Aren't achievement and prosperity in a dominantly white world a needed demonstration to other blacks that *it can be done*, that a black in America can "eat lobsters" and live the good life? Besides, the accumulation of economic or political power by African-American achievers, if properly used, obviously might contribute to the betterment of blacks generally. As Charles Hamilton pointed out, Vernon Jordan is the first black to have become "a legitimate national power broker"—indeed a "qualitatively different" black achievement.

About neighborhoods where "most families do not have a steadily employed breadwinner," however, William Julius Wilson has cogently argued a conflicting view. In such areas crime, hanging out, alienation, resulting in prostitution, drug addiction, and imprisonment, have increased and probably will keep on increasing. In some measure the departure of successful African-Americans and the consequent isolation of inner-city youth may be responsible.[7]

So the personal success of those African-Americans who have moved out of the ghetto and into the middle class or beyond it might not be a *racial* success at all, when measured against the worsening plight of the inner city.

All this is undoubtedly the subject of much concern among

affluent African-Americans. Have they left "their people" behind? If so, can that be justified by personal success? If not, how do they maintain the needed racial solidarity while retaining the good lives they have made for themselves and their families and believe themselves entitled to enjoy?

No less a black hero than Earvin "Magic" Johnson, the great basketball player whose career was cut short by HIV, has warned today's black youth that they must compete in what is still in most ways a white world. Johnson grew up in Lansing, Michigan, one of the ten children of a cafeteria worker and a father who held two jobs. Visiting Southwestern, a mostly black high school in Detroit in 1993, he told attentive students bluntly that "the odds are against any of you making it."

The odds had been against him too, he recalled, but "I loved the challenge. . . . Tell me I can't do it and I say, 'We'll see about that.'" He went on:

> When I was in the tenth grade I could only read at an eighth-grade level. I was told I had to go to summer school to bring that up [or] I'd never be able to play basketball in college. My guys told me, "Aw, Earvin, what you goin' to summer school for? Hang out with us on the street." But I had a goal. I said "Come on with me to summer school. Hang with me there." I went two summers and by the time I was in the eleventh grade I was reading at college level.

Johnson is now paid ten million dollars a year, following a successful basketball career at Michigan State and with the Los Angeles Lakers. He's reported to be a potential buyer of a National Basketball Association franchise. As he was leaving Southwestern, he made his own point about the middle class and the underclass and offered a piece of professional advice to Jalen Rose, a Southwestern graduate, then a basketball star at the University of Michigan.

"Keep giving back to the community," the six-foot ten-inch Magic said to the six-foot nine-inch Rose, "and take advantage of the smaller guards."[8]

*   *   *

Randall Kennedy, an African-American law professor at Harvard, once listened in on a family argument between his father and his brother.[9] The elder Kennedy believed that a black person could succeed in America only by "selling out" to white society. The son insisted, in reply, that his father's belief was tantamount to a concession that blacks were not as capable as whites and could not "make it" on their own. Blacks, he insisted, *could* get ahead, even in white society, by skill, brains, and hard work.

Their dispute raises the question of what, in racial terms, *is* "a sellout." An African-American clearly would have a difficult task succeeding materially in American society (save perhaps in sports or show biz) without joining, to some extent, in the values and attitudes of that society—as a minor example, without dressing conventionally. Would that be a sellout? Or only a sensible adaptation to reality? Or is even the acceptance of what is, instead of what ought to be, a sellout?

Randall Kennedy, himself a leader in his chosen, mostly white field, seemed to come down more nearly on the side of his brother. With some amusement he recalled that his father (not apparently a man to be trifled with) thought him "a fool" to be a college professor when, with his education and ability, he probably could have done much better economically and had more power in some other role.

If the question of what *is* a sellout is a dilemma for adult blacks, it must be agonizing for that traditionally anxious cohort, teenagers, specifically black teenagers. Contempt for "acting white," for example, is a phenomenon noted among them by scholars like Ronald Ferguson of the Malcolm Wiener Center for Social Policy at Harvard.

Surveying some Texas school districts, Ferguson found repeated patterns of black student behavior: boys' academic performance falling off by the seventh grade and falling farther by the ninth; girls' performance slipping to the level of the boys' in the ninth grade; after that, the girls "leveling off" and the boys falling farther behind.[10] Teachers tended to see these black learning patterns as fitting their stereotypes of less capable black pupils. Ferguson believes instead that the patterns actually reflect the black youth culture.

As he explains, black youths perceive things about themselves that they like better than their perceptions (stereotypes) of whites. They don't like to see blacks doing "white things," like speaking proper English, and they don't appreciate whites who try to do "black things," like making rap music. Only the occasional exception is admitted. Larry Byrd, even if white, was an obvious star in basketball, regarded as *the* black game, and Vernon Jordan, even if black, obviously is at the top of the white world.

Stereotypes, however, tend to enforce their opposites. Black youths think that only blacks can leap above the rim in basketball,* but they concede that whites do good schoolwork. So in their minds the opposites also tend to be true: Whites do good schoolwork but can't jump; blacks can jump but can't do good schoolwork. An "antiachievement" pressure is thus at work, and even gifted black pupils, as responsive to peer pressures as any other young people, sometimes succumb rather than be accused of acting white.

This antiachievement phenomenon seems more than unfortunate. Speaking proper English, doing well in school are virtually prerequisite for making it in what is still a white world. But black youths, like most adolescents, often prefer the approval of street-talking peers to that of their parents or teachers or some vague idea of a future employer.

In the case of academic achievement, unlike wearing their baseball caps backward or their Nikes unlaced, young African-Americans could be handicapping themselves for life—at least as whites see it. But to youthful blacks, refusing to act white is an assertion of their own independence, values, and pride, blackness unbending in a white world.

* * *

*The seriocomic movie *White Men Can't Jump* was based on this stereotype.

Randall Kennedy believes that all middle-class blacks feel some degree of black guilt at being more fortunate than others and that it's this guilt that triggers manifestations of black pride by black college students on formerly white campuses, particularly wealthy and coveted campuses like Harvard and Yale.

African-American students at such institutions, as Kennedy has observed them, are likely to be on scholarships or to come from affluent families, good high schools, or private schools. Some are affirmative action beneficiaries. These students feel deeply that they are privileged in comparison with so many African-Americans of their generation "hanging out" on ghetto street corners and headed for prison, prostitution, drugs—or all three.

Thus black student actions that to whites seem hostile—isolating themselves from nonblack students, issuing "demands," staging demonstrations against real or perceived white dominance—often are attempts by favored blacks to show themselves as well as their inner-city "brothers and sisters" that they are black as well as privileged—not "sellouts."

White students and faculty, particularly alumni and alumnae, tend to think, however, that a black student at Stanford or Princeton or any other prestigious campus should be grateful for the privilege—at least not be hostile to his or her surroundings. John Hope Franklin would recognize the condescending undercurrent: What do these people *want*? Haven't we done enough for them? Isn't just being at Ivy League U more than most of them could have expected not too long ago?

Black student demonstrations and militant black rhetoric, even if derived from black guilt, puzzle and anger whites. This causes a stiffening of black attitudes toward the perceived "racism" of the response, which in turn heightens white reaction, and the situation typically escalates into charge and counter-charge, sometimes by belligerents from off the campus (often inflammatory coverage in the press), until what may have been a relatively minor incident or demand has become a full-fledged racial confrontation, with divisive consequences.

Something like that happened in the early nineties at my alma mater, the "liberal" University of North Carolina. UNC has twenty-one hundred black students and claims fourteen endowed black professors out of a national total of sixty-one. A largely noncontroversial plan for an expanded black cultural center on campus became a heated battle over black student demands for the BCC to be housed not in an addition to an existing facility but in a "free-standing building." After many loud debates and demonstrations by both sides, the university agreed to the separate building, though not without angry dissent from white faculty, alumni, and students.

It remains to be seen, at this writing, whether the ultimate result will be a more isolated and racially separate black student body, as critics contend, or whether, in the words of Provost Richard McCormick, "the process of settling the [black cultural center] issue can provide Carolina with the opportunity to create a new era in race relations at our University."[11]

Originally the BCC controversy may have been more nearly an effort to assuage the guilt feelings of black students than a deliberate expression of black-white hostility, though that's what it became. However that may be, the episode reflects—years after the nation's supposed "integration"—the lack of understanding and respect that continues to plague the relations of white Americans and even middle-class African-Americans.

African-American journalists, by definition, are part of the middle class. Like white journalists, they may not be paid as well as doctors or business executives, but by education, interest, and occupation, sometimes even by influence on events, they are among those African-Americans who have "made it."

There are, however, few black managing editors, black business editors, black sports editors (see Chapter Twelve), black fashion writers, black critics (though in 1995 Margo Jefferson of *The New York Times* won a Pulitzer Prize for her critical articles). In all the daily operations of the American press, from coverage of foreign news to reporting on domestic elections, black sensibility, black insight, black understanding, and black experience are notable mainly for their lack.

Black participation in the control and management of publishing and broadcasting for the great majority of Americans is virtually nil, and in 1995 a federal appeals court blocked, at least temporarily, an effort by the Federal Communications Commission to ease African-American entry into the lucrative new fields of wireless telephone and data services. Publishing and broadcasting primarily for blacks are fields with an obviously limited market.

More than six thousand minority journalists, representing blacks, Hispanics, Asians, and Native Americans, met in Atlanta in 1994. The executives sent to speak to them by the nation's most influential and prestigious news organizations were almost all white since few blacks are at that level of journalism.

The opening passages of a study by the National Association of Black Journalists reflect the symbolic situation that results:

> African-American journalists and the bosses of their newsrooms are operating in different worlds. . . . [The] journalists see supervisors setting unrealistic standards for them. The managers, most of whom were white, say that lack of experience and skills of black journalists are more serious hurdles than any application of a double standard. . . . [12]

These contrasting views (it hardly matters, in this context, which is correct; probably neither is wholly so) make the situation of African-American journalists (blacks in a dominantly white institution) virtually a mirror of the situation of African-Americans generally (blacks in a dominantly white society). *Neither side sees the same institution, the same society, as the other.*

Of the African-American journalists, 67 percent said their superiors were not "committed to retaining and promoting black journalists." But 94 percent of newsroom managers said their organizations had a "serious commitment" to that goal. "Differences in culture and background" were a cause of black underrepresentation in the press, according to 79 percent of NABJ members. Only 59 percent of white managers agreed.

Why don't blacks move up in the newsroom? Lack of experience, said 71 percent of managers. Only 41 percent of the black journalists agreed. And 92 percent of managers but only 28 percent of the blacks said promotion standards were the same for blacks and whites; 59 percent of the NABJ members said blacks "have to meet higher standards."

As for "career opportunities," 97 percent of managers said blacks were "as or more likely than" whites to get a chance for promotion. Only 24 percent of NABJ members thought so. Of the latter, 60 percent said they weren't even equally informed of career opportunities. And 67 percent said blacks had to spend more time than whites in entry-level jobs, while only 12 percent of managers agreed.

On only one question did white managers and black journalists see more or less eye to eye. A high percentage of both thought that "the lack of mentors and role models" was a "serious problem" for black journalists. Whites apparently can't fill or aren't filling that important need. Echoing a feminist complaint, one black journalist said others in the newsroom were "all white males who don't get it and moreover are terrified of African-American men."

It's not to be supposed that these perceptions, on either side, are entirely objective. Black journalists have obvious reasons for seeing bias where there may be little or none; white managers have a clear stake in seeing their organizations and themselves as making good-faith efforts toward racial equality, whatever others may think.

The stark differences reflected in the NABJ survey can't be easily dismissed, however. The mere fact that most of the managers were white is significant, both for a press in which the black community is underrepresented and for black journalists who—for whatever reason—have rarely moved into positions of management, control, or influence. To the extent that press coverage may be distorted or inaccurate or insensitive or merely inadequate, owing to a weak or nonexistent black presence in the newsroom and in news managers' offices, the general public, including white persons, is also the poorer.

What is really striking in the survey of journalists, however, is the startling lack of a common understanding between the races: blacks pointing to unfair treatment, whites citing black deficiencies, for the same unhappy consequences. Even decades after the end of legal segregation, would not a comparable survey of the larger black and white communities disclose much the same wide, perhaps unbridgeable gulf between the America that blacks see and the America in which whites believe both races live?

12 Speeches and Spokesmen

... the ravings of an obscure hate merchant at a campus remote from the limelight.

New York Times *editorial*

At a public budget meeting in Deer Park, New York, in October 1993, Assessor Josephine Kent complained that the state comptroller was no longer reimbursing towns for supplying his office with data on taxes and property assessments.

"That's since Carl McCall was appointed from the city of New York," Town Councilman Joseph Kover said. "The nigger from Harlem."

Wayne Decker, another councilman, quickly interjected: "Hey, Joe, you're in a public meeting."

"I am telling you what he is," Kover said, and repeated the epithet. Questioned later, he defended it: "It means a black man, period. I don't think it's offensive."

Carl McCall did. So did Governor Mario Cuomo, who had appointed McCall comptroller. So did a number of Deer Park residents who called for Kover, a former state welfare fraud inspector, to resign. He refused and remained on the Town Council and the Orange County Republican Committee. On November 13, 1993, weeks after his remarks at the budget meeting,

Kover finally apologized to Comptroller McCall but stayed on both panels.

The New York Times ran two stories on this incident, both inside the paper, with what it calls a "shirttail," a brief addition, to one saying that McCall had accepted Kover's apology.

At about the same time, on the highly rated CBS program *60 Minutes*, General Carl Mundy, Jr., the commandant of the Marine Corps, observed that "in the military skills, we find that the minority officers do not shoot as well as the non-minorities.... They don't swim as well. And when you give them a compass and send them across the terrain at night ... they don't do as well. ..."

Mundy apologized the next day. The Marine Corps, however, later released records purportedly supporting his remark. David Banks, an associate professor of statistics at Carnegie-Mellon University, said the performance differentials cited by corps spokesmen were not statistically significant. And Edwin Dorn, the Defense Department's highest personnel official, said that "the one bit of data that is bothersome to us" in an analysis of Marine officer selections in 1993 was that "minorities and particularly blacks appear less likely to get promoted from captain to major than are whites."

The *Times* published nothing on Mundy's televised remarks but ran a short wire service report of his apology. The *Los Angeles Times* ran its story on page 41. The New York *Daily News* ran a page 2 news story on the remark itself, with an editorial calling it "outrageous." The *60 Minutes* program did not publicize the matter. *The Washington Post* did not report Mundy's broadcast words but later ran a full account of the incident, Mundy's apology, the Marine Corps statistical release, and the statements by Banks and Dorn.[1]

On November 29, 1993, before an audience variously reported as "about 140" and "several dozen" students of Kean College in Union, New Jersey, a representative of the Nation of Islam, Khalid Abdul Muhammad, delivered an appalling diatribe against Jews—"the bloodsuckers of the black nation"—the pope, homosexuals, the disabled, even some other blacks. For about three hours Muhammad raved on, mentioning Columbia "Jew-niversity" in "Jew York City" and claiming that Jews had brought the Holocaust on themselves.

Muhammad reserved his bloodthirstiest call for blacks who might someday take political control in South Africa, advising them to kill all whites who remained there for twenty-four hours after the takeover—"and when you get through killing them all, go to the goddamn graveyard and dig up the grave and kill them a-goddamn-gain because they didn't die hard enough."

A tape of Muhammad's outburst recorded some laughter and applause from the audience of mostly black students. But one African-American youth stood up and told Khalid that his speech recalled Hitler's Third Reich. Khalid replied that the young man looked like "a damn Tom." This exchange did not receive wide notice until a year later, when it was reported in a column by Colbert I. King on the op-ed page of *The Washington Post,* on December 16, 1995.

For a week after Khalid's speech, nothing happened. The college administration's silence outraged a white professor, Jay L. Spaulding, who had been in the audience under the impression that Kean's black studies program was to be discussed. What he heard instead, he wrote the college's board of trustees, was "a display of racist and sectarian stupidity . . . cultist garbage. . . ."

The administration's silence after Muhammad's ferocious speech also upset Governor-elect Christine Whitman and the New Jersey chancellor for higher education, Dr. Edward D. Goldberg. Whitman denounced Muhammad and sponsored a public seminar on tolerance. Dr. Goldberg wrote the college president, Dr. Elsa Gomez, on December 10, 1993, criticizing her and the trustees for failing to counter "patently racist ideas and opinions delivered in a campus setting."

By then, on December 9, Dr. Gomez had publicly condemned Muhammad's remarks as "filled with verbal abuse and expressions of hate." But she specified that even such odious views were constitutionally protected speech.

Sharp exchanges followed between Drs. Gomez and Goldberg and between Dr. Henry Kaplowitz, president of the Jewish Faculty and Staff Associates, and James Conyers, assistant director of the African studies program. Other faculty and students were drawn into the acrimony, roiling the campus and deepening tensions in a student body of twelve thousand (of whom 14 percent were black or Hispanic at the time, and 1 percent Jewish).

Still, the matter was mostly a local issue, little remarked outside New Jersey, until, on December 29, a full month after Muhammad had spoken at Kean, *The New York Times* published an account of the controversy. Even then the *Times*, apparently unexcited by the story, had held it for a week, since it was datelined December 22.* The article by Jon Nordheimer, moreover, was less devoted to a speech delivered nearly a month earlier than to the resulting controversy on the Kean campus and between Drs. Gomez and Goldberg.

Publication of Nordheimer's story set off a slowly gathering storm. On January 8, on the *Times* op-ed page, Roger Wilkins, the African-American history professor at George Mason University, bluntly accused Kean's black faculty members of "avoiding swift and forceful condemnation of Mr. Muhammad's bilious diatribe." In ducking that obligation, Wilkins wrote, they had "failed their obligations as members of a civilized community and failed to uphold the best traditions of the black struggle."

Such well-targeted criticism as Wilkins's soon escalated, however, into broader demands for black repudiation of Muhammad and his poisonous views. Three days after Wilkins's article, in a column in the *Times*, A. M. Rosenthal declared that "from almost all of America's black political and intellectual leadership [Muhammad] received something even more valuable to him and other black peddlers of hatred: silence about the growth of anti-Semitism."

"Almost all of America's black political and intellectual leadership" probably had had no knowledge of Muhammad's speech

---

*The *Times* has a policy of dating a story on the day it was written, no matter how long it might be held before publication.

since the *Times* itself had published nothing about it until a month had passed. Rosenthal's column, appearing on January 11, was almost six weeks after the fact.

Nor did the columnist explain why other black leaders had to take responsibility for Muhammad's abhorrent views. Does the white president of, say, Harvard, owe an apology to blacks for the racial views of white academics like William Shockley? The national Republican party did not accept responsibility for David Duke, the ex-Klansman who was nearly elected governor of Louisiana as a Republican, nor did anyone demand that it do so.

Yet as news of Muhammad's speech gained currency, it was widely asserted that the intemperate remarks of a second-rank official of an extremist group, made to a small audience at an obscure campus and not even widely circulated for more than a month, would stand as representative of African-American opinion *unless* black leaders repudiated every aspect of it.

Richard Cohen, a columnist for *The Washington Post*, joined Rosenthal in demanding that black leaders repudiate Muhammad. On January 16 the Anti-Defamation League of B'nai B'rith paid for a full-page ad in *The New York Times*, quoting some of Muhammad's excrescences. The ADL also provided journalists with a tape recording of his speech.

Black leaders got the message. William Gray, the former congressman from Pennsylvania who heads the United Negro College Fund, declared: "At no time can we tolerate racism and anti-Semitism, nor can it be justified as a response to repression." Jesse Jackson called the Muhammad speech "racist, anti-Semitic, divisive, untrue and chilling," all of which it had been for nearly two months, during most of which Jackson might well have had no inkling of what Muhammad had said. Benjamin Chavis, then the executive director of the NAACP, said he was "appalled that any human being would stoop so low to make such violence-prone anti-Semitic comments."

Charles Rangel, the African-American congressman from Harlem, said more sensibly that "clearly, we're dealing with a person [Muhammad] who is very dangerous, bitter and, in my opinion, very sick"—*not, however*, someone who spoke for the black community as a whole.

Sydney Schanberg of *New York Newsday* weighed in on January 25 in a column quoting from the ADL tape and noting with approval that the Muhammad controversy "has finally made its way into national print, putting pressure on mainstream black leaders to repudiate the hate message." The next day a *Times* editorial called it "encouraging that, as the contents of the speech have become widely known, responsible black political and organization leaders have risen to deplore and denounce it." Neither Schanberg nor the *Times* editorial said *why* "responsible" black leaders should be under such pressure or why it was "encouraging" that they were succumbing.

Another resounding blow was struck by Representative Kweisi Mfume, the Maryland Democrat who then headed the Congressional Black Caucus. He had announced that the caucus was exploring the idea of working with the Nation of Islam, until then a group isolated among black leaders but with a substantial membership in the black community.

Publicity about Muhammad's speech at Kean blew Mfume's plans right out of the water. Under pressure from Black Caucus members, he announced on February 2 that the group would back away from any working relationship with the Nation of Islam and, implicitly, from the view of a growing number of African-Americans that greater unity among black groups was needed for an attack on the problems of the inner city.

That same day the Senate of the United States condemned Muhammad's speech in a formal resolution adopted 97–0. The resolution was cosponsored by Senators Edward Kennedy, Democrat of Massachusetts, and John Danforth, Republican of Missouri. No one mentioned, in floor debate, General Mundy's reservations about black Marine officers or the recent wisecrack by Senator Ernest Hollings, Democrat of South Carolina and a former presidential candidate, that African leaders went to international trade conferences to "get a good square meal" instead of "eating each other." Nor did any senator recall the statement of Senator Alfonse D'Amato, Republican of New York, that he would not reply to Hollings because "I have too many important things to do." Both Hollings and D'Amato voted for the resolution to condemn Muhammad.

Ultimately the late-breaking storm of reaction to Muhammad's speech caused even Louis Farrakhan of the Nation of Islam to retreat far enough to add to Muhammad's new fame. Farrakhan removed him as his national assistant and called the Kean speech "meanspirited"—but refused to dissociate himself from unspecified "truths" he said Muhammad had uttered.

Muhammad's vitriol, for which he was paid $2,650 from student, not state, funds, was far more intemperate, inflammatory, and absurd than anything said by Hollings, Mundy, or Joseph Kover. No one who condemned Muhammad for his speech was in the wrong. Quite the opposite. His views were execrable and in some cases factually wrong. But they were *his*, not those of the overall black community, not even, as subsequent events showed, those of most African-Americans at Kean. The best response would have been for his speech to have been sensibly countered— not censored—by the Kean College faculty and administration soon after it was delivered, perhaps at a conference of reputable white and black persons from on and off the campus.

The columnists who demanded that blacks repudiate the speech, the number of blacks who did so, the ADL's full-page ad, the Black Caucus's rejection of the Nation of Islam, the U.S. Senate's official condemnation—all long after the objectionable words were heard by that small audience in Union, New Jersey—called attention to the speech that it would not otherwise have received or deserved and gave it an importance that no rational analysis can support. Black leaders' ritual condemnation of a speech neither they nor most Americans had even known about for more than a month left the impression that Muhammad's diatribe had been a significant statement of African-American views, an idea for which there is no evidence beyond the recorded laughter and applause in the taped response of a small student audience that had invited Muhammad in the first place.

Rosenthal charged in the *Times* that there was "a surge of anti-Semitism and anti-Semitic propaganda among blacks, particularly among young and more educated blacks." He gave no evidence to support that statement, even though there *are* indications of a "rise," if not a "surge." But after the hype that followed Muhammad's speech, much of white America may well believe that anti-Semitism is welling up in every African-American breast.

Rosenthal also said in his January 11 article that he himself had "heard casual anti-Semitism from black achievers." No doubt he has, but is there a white person in America who has not heard "casual" antiblack words spoken by other whites in country club locker rooms, expensive restaurants, or local diners, on the assembly line or the grocery checkout line, by police officers, professors, in newsrooms, on the street, on the job, in taxicabs, almost anywhere, almost anytime, by almost anybody?

Some African-Americans probably do harbor resentments and even hatreds that Muhammad put into despicable words. But some whites often have used Joseph Kover's choice of epithets too. In the case of Muhammad, that *Times* editorial had it right when it first declared that it was tempting "to dismiss this diatribe as the ravings of an obscure hate-merchant at a campus remote from the limelight." Exactly.

Unfortunately, on second thought, the *Times* decided the speech was "unnerving" and went on to join a general chorus that left an all-too-clear implication: that an African-American making hateful remarks about whites is more to be deplored and denounced than whites making racist or insulting remarks about blacks.

The Kean College episode was an instance among many of the American press's tendency to ignore or play down significant events until developments force them into notice.

Even the civil rights movements of the fifties and sixties did not really make the headlines until it developed colorful spokesmen like Martin Luther King and met flamboyant opponents like George Wallace. The movement could hardly have hoped for better publicity than Bull Connor handed it with his cattle prods or for more sympathy than white Mississippians created by murdering Medgar Evers and civil rights workers in 1964.

Even environmentalism got short shrift in the press, compared with orthodox business views, until the huge outpouring of public interest that greeted the first Earth Day in 1970. Stories about sexism and feminism were hardly to be found in news columns or broadcasts until women started burning their bras. "Sexual harassment" went mostly unmentioned until Anita Hill came forward in 1991 to testify on television against Clarence Thomas, a Supreme Court nominee. Consumerism got the necessary boost into press consciousness only from Ralph Nader's one-man campaign against the automakers. Until gays came "out of the closet" into public demonstrations and marches, the press took little notice of their existence. And only after the bombing of the Oklahoma City federal building in 1995 did the press wake up to the presence of numerous armed antigovernment "militias" readying themselves for a shoot-out with their paranoid conception of "a new world order."

When the press belatedly focused on the dramatic civil rights movement, a development of far greater long-term effect went virtually unnoticed: the great post–World War II migration of African-Americans out of the sharecropper shacks of the South into Harlem and Baltimore and Chicago and Detroit.

This movement had no obvious heroes or villains. Whites did not meet blacks at the city limits with tear gas. Robed Klansmen did not lynch passengers on the Illinois Central who sought good jobs in the North and fled agricultural mechanization in the South. But Nicholas Lemann later described what was happening as

[one] of the largest and most rapid mass internal movements of people . . . perhaps the greatest migration not caused by the immediate threat of execution or starvation. In sheer numbers, it

outranks the migration of any other ethnic group—Italians or Irish or Jews or Poles—to this country. And it radically changed the racial landscape of America.[2]

Yet this protracted and cataclysmic migration, unfolding over decades, representing an upheaval comparable to that of the Civil War, went virtually unnoticed in the American press, even in the cities most affected, until in the sixties and seventies the subject could no longer be avoided because of the discovery of a prime result: the inner-city underclass.

Over the years when the nation most needed to be alerted to the vast change inevitably coming about, the press was paying virtually no attention. That immensely consequential default is perhaps being repeated today, as the cities of America are becoming "Latinized" by an influx of immigrants, legal and illegal, from Hispanic nations—the Watts area of Los Angeles, for instance, the scene of the 1967 race riots, becoming mostly Latino and only 5 percent black.[3]

Such vast human movements present little drama of the kind the Bull Connors of this world create. They are the kinds of events—more trend than happening—the American press is not well equipped to report or even to recognize (the anti-immigrant Prop 187 *did* get heavy coverage in 1994 because it was involved in California's senatorial and gubernatorial campaigns).

The American press, moreover, is more reliant than it likes to admit on spokesmen—not just representatives of a movement or an institution, like King or Nader, who can themselves be covered, but actual press agents and "information officers," important titleholders in important organizations, and elected politicians and their appointed staffs. An automobile company executive, for example, can quickly get coverage for his views on foreign trade if he's well known and his company matters, although his views may be ignorant and bigoted or commonplace, or all three.

Such spokesmen, mostly because they're official, usually can get space or airtime for routine, self-serving, or misleading information when less impressive, less well-connected, less "official" persons cannot get the press to pay attention to something that may be more important or immediate.

The best newspapers and broadcasters can sometimes be defeated by the "dailiness" of things, today's earthquake coming before news of yesterday's hurricane has been properly digested. Millions of words and images pouring into newsrooms on wizard communications devices have to be sorted into news columns or thirty-minute broadcasts, under daunting time pressures. Official spokesmen, in these circumstances, can sometimes be indispensable.

The most sophisticated of them know how to take full advantage of news organization needs they are only too anxious to fill. Those relied on by the press, however, seldom include African-Americans—except those asked to talk about specifically African-American affairs. Thus a black educator might be asked to defend affirmative action or a black social worker to talk about welfare. A few African-Americans—Colin Powell, Donald McHenry, Condoleezza Rice—qualify by experience as spokespersons on foreign affairs, but in general, those called upon by press and television for expert opinion are senior and official, hence white. Inevitably the press reflects these spokesmen's views and sensibilities.

Reporters, moreover, tend to learn what they know about their subject from the spokesmen they cover on the beat. These "sources" too, with rare exceptions, tend to be official, senior, and white. This frequently imparts to the news a "spin" reflecting the interests of the organization or institution represented by the spokesman and almost never known to the reader or viewer.

Decades ago I wrote a book review column for the Winston-Salem Sunday *Journal and Sentinel*. A readership survey disclosed that my book column was read by one half of 1 percent of the paper's circulation. The column therefore was scheduled for extinction. I went to Reed Sarratt, the executive editor, and argued passionately that that particular one half of 1 percent of our readers probably included the most thoughtful, most civic-minded people in town. Didn't we want the *Journal and Sentinel* to appeal to them? Sarratt agreed, not happily, and granted my column a reprieve.

That probably would not happen today. Polltaking, ratings measurements, readership surveys have become so much a tool of the trade that nothing prevails against them. TV's relentless quest for high ratings, once the curse of the entertainment shows, now has infected network and particularly local news broadcasts too. Newspapers, less obviously, also have been seized by the ratings—in their case, readership—fever. Not the least result is that the news, in whatever medium, now tends to be "down-market"—heavy on sex, sensationalism, and sin.

The very presence of television cameras, moreover—a phenomenon of less than half a century—has changed both the news and the coverage of the news. During the 1967 riots in Los Angeles, television coverage *declined* as the riots continued, but as the 1992 riots went on, TV coverage *increased*.[4] This no doubt reflected viewers' choice; they wanted to see what was happening and expected TV to satisfy their desires. But it may well have extended the violence as rioters sought to use alarmed TV viewers as one of their weapons, a strategy not well understood in the sixties. Thus TV covered the riots and the riots continued because TV covered them. But had the cameras been removed, the viewing public would have been outraged.

The nightly crime story has become a regular feature of local television, particularly if the crime was violent. Editors and broadcast executives insist that polls show overpowering public concern about crime, particularly black crime; so, they say, they are only responding. No doubt, but might not the TV emphasis on crime have the reciprocal effect of causing viewers to tell polltakers they are concerned about crime? And influencing them to think of crime as *black* crime?

On the other hand, thoughtful discussion of such matters as imprisonment, sentencing policies, the "war on drugs," the understaffing of criminal justice agencies, or police tactics is rare in newspapers and especially on television. Such dull stuff is reserved mostly for op-ed articles and low-rated documentaries, while the headlines and the nightly news concentrate on heinous crime, weeping survivors, depraved villains, fearful citizenry—drama. The idea of economic and social causes of crime, if mentioned at all, is usually derided as bleeding-heart liberalism or egghead scholars' nonsense—especially by the politicians and police officials that tel evision and newspapers feature as spokesmen and "experts."

In too many cases, moreover, both broadcast and print press indulges a rage to simplify that flagrantly *over*simplifies and even distorts conflicts and issues. The Los Angeles riots of 1992, for example, were widely reported as blacks vs. whites, an idea easily grasped by a public accustomed to racial conflict. Reporters and editors, moreover, were still fighting "the last war": the black-white riots of the sixties that many also had covered.

In 1992, therefore, African-Americans were given greater prominence than any other racial group: The first or "top of the news" story on television featured blacks in 49 percent of cases, Latinos in only 13 percent. Blacks accounted for 43 percent of sound bites aired as against only 8 percent for Latinos. Yet 51 percent of those arrested by the Los Angeles Police Department were Latinos. Only 38 percent were black; 9 percent were white.[5]

Hearing these figures presented at the Kennedy School of Government at Harvard in 1993, Lee Smith, a former *New York Times* reporter, spoke up in some heat: "Washington Heights in New York is now heavily Latino, particularly Dominican. But the New York media thought it was still black until there was a Dominican riot over the death of a drug dealer. Many in the media still think of Washington Heights as an area where German refugees settled before World War II."

An aide to Raymond Flynn, the mayor of Boston in 1993, chimed in to say that neighborhoods and leaders were inadequately depicted in the Boston press too, with the result that "whites don't know or understand what's happening in these communities. They don't understand the rage that permeates them."[6]

That is a serious charge, tantamount to saying that the American press is presenting a one-sided—or at least inadequate—picture of the American society it supposedly covers. That's seldom conceded in the newsroom, and almost never intended, but all too often true.

13 Tragic Failure

We want our birthright! We want our place at
the table with other Americans.

Glenn Loury

Susan Smith was in tune with the racism in society. She knew what would work best to direct attention away from her: point the finger at a
black man.

Dr. Alvin Poussaint

David Kim, the president of the Korean Grocers Association
of Los Angeles, was deeply involved in 1992 in that city's
riots, which resulted less from black-white hostilities than from
ethnic rivalries turning into violence. Kim later was invited to
speak about the riots at the Kennedy School of Government at
Harvard.

He proved to be an articulate *engineer*, who told his audience
how he had earned the necessary degrees and license for that
profession before leaving Korea. In the United States, confronted
with the need for American credentials, he found it easier and
quicker to go into the grocery business. Talking to Kim after
his remarks, I found him more at home in the Harvard atmosphere than almost any transplanted southern black would have

been, or any African-American born and reared in the inner city.

Immigrants like Kim often are better able to "make it" in competitive America than native-born blacks. As such immigrants surge ahead economically—Koreans have virtually taken over, for instance, the independent fruit and vegetable stores of New York City—impatient white Americans often ask: Why don't American blacks do as well?

African-Americans, the questioners seem not to realize, are carrying lifelong burdens of discrimination and disdain, as did their parents and ancestors. These burdens, commonly overlooked by whites, are seldom understood by immigrants either. Most of them had their own problems in the countries they left, and many therefore find life in America liberating and hopeful, the antithesis of the life experience of most native-born blacks.

Their American experience is "what is different for my people," Jesse Jackson has written. Angered by an interviewer's suggestion that "many of these immigrant groups have leap-frogged over [blacks] and walked through the door that James Meredith* and others pushed open in the Sixties," Jackson retorted that immigrants had not shared blacks' "history of discrimination . . . [and] did not engage in the confrontation for change. They simply benefited from the role we play[ed] as warriors. . . . How many other ethnic groups have marched down that highway, got beat up on the Edmund Pettus Bridge in Selma, Alabama for the right to vote?"[1]

William Julius Wilson points out another difference, numbers: "[I]f you were to open the flood gates and let tens of millions [of Asians] into America, then you would see similar problems to those of the black community. . . . Look at . . . Chinatowns in

---

*James Meredith was the first black student at the University of Mississippi. His forced enrollment there in 1963 caused bloodshed and death, in one of the notable events of the Kennedy administration.

New York and San Francisco—gangs, drugs, crime and violence. . . . That hardly holds to the stereotype of . . . industrious paragons of Confucian virtue."[2]

Dr. Allen Counter, a faculty biologist who also heads Harvard University's Foundation for Intercultural Relations, has in his office a large model of a monument—someday to be erected in Washington, D.C.—commemorating the black experience in America. Those who inspect the model see a depiction of the hold of a slave ship with naked blacks packed in like sardines, lying side by side, head to foot, in chains.[3]

That's not what most whites and no doubt many blacks want to commemorate or even remember, but blacks did not come to these shores as voluntary immigrants to a land of promise. They had been kidnapped, sold like cattle, chained in the noisome holds of slave ships, bound for a future of burden and sorrow. And unlike the immigrants of recent decades, blacks have been here *from the start*.

Roger Wilkins has described the origins of the black experience in America:

> Black people were not brought here in the holds of ships as cattle, as chattel, in inhuman conditions because white people just wanted to be mean. Or because the Christian god required white people to do that. Or because white people had this monstrous need to feel psychically better than a group of other people. They did it for money!
>
> They had a wilderness to tame and crops to grow and they needed energy. They didn't have bulldozers. Didn't have wheat pickers. White indentured servants could slip away and be lost in the crowd. Native Americans died. So they found black people in Africa. It was about money.[4]

Blacks were carried unwillingly into Virginia as early as the seventeenth century, and thereafter they and their descendants helped build the nation. They fought in its Revolution and in the Civil War for their own freedom. They tilled America's fields, drove its cattle across the West, died in its Indian wars, nursed its children, shared in its ills, if seldom its glories, made in their music perhaps the greatest American contribution to world culture, and sustained more staunchly than any other population group the nation's largely Christian faith.

Nathan Irvin Huggins, the Harvard historian, made the crucial distinction that by heritage, most of those who call themselves African-Americans today are fundamentally *Americans*. They are not, Huggins pointed out, "alien" immigrants but an "alienated" population, mostly "Protestant and English-speaking, sharing more of the culture of the Anglo-Saxon majority than any" immigrants (more, certainly, than Asians or Latins) and with "historic claims to birthright citizenship."[5]

One afternoon at Boston University, as I talked with the African-American economist Glenn Loury, he angrily pounded the table, insisting: "We don't want assimilation! We want our birthright! We want our place at the table with other Americans."[6]

African-Americans have a right to that place at the table. But as natives of this country they sometimes recoil from the idea that like newcomers, they should be glad to get any job, no matter how menial or ill paid, in order to advance themselves and become "American." Nicholas Lemann has pointed out that the willingness of today's native blacks "to participate in the world at the bottom rung and to put up with just about anything" is not as high as was that of their parents' and grandparents' in the years when the latter were migrating from the South to the big cities.[7]

African-Americans think and react, in other words, more like *other Americans* than like the newly arrived immigrants—Koreans, Vietnamese, Mexicans—with whom they are erroneously compared. They *are* Americans. Few whites, however, understand this compelling fact of black Americans' history: *They have been here as long as whites have*, longer than most.

That's why Lincoln was unable to persuade nineteenth-century black leaders to accept colonization in Central America or Liberia. America was their home as much as his. That's what led African-Americans in this century to demand equal status in the armed forces, including combat duty, when discriminatory treatment in the past might have caused them to resist fighting and dying for a nation that had used them so badly.

More important today, the passionate belief that they are "fully American" explains why African-Americans continue, even after legal desegregation, to claim that white prejudice cheats them of something rightfully theirs, something that whites have no standing to "give" them, something blacks should not have to "earn" in the marketplace, a birthright, what Huggins called "a historic claim to being sharing partners in the commonwealth."

Thirty years after sweeping civil rights legislation was enacted in the sixties, however, it's clear that white America does not recognize that claim and refuses still to accept African-Americans as "sharing partners" in the land of the free.

In the first month of 1995, nearly half a century after the Supreme Court ruled that school segregation was unconstitutional, the issue again came before a different Supreme Court. The state of Missouri argued that it had met its court-imposed obligation to end segregation in the Kansas City school system, even though student achievement in the district had shown no improvement since desegregation was ordered in 1986.

Educational success was irrelevant, argued John R. Munich, Missouri's assistant attorney general. All that mattered, he told the Court, was whether the state had complied with court orders to assure that pupil assignments to schools and resource allocations to the district and between its schools were nondiscriminatory.

Justice David Souter asked if it might not be "a fact or a relevant consideration" that the years of school segregation in Kansas City before 1986 had had "an effect on attitudes and expectations that get passed on from one school generation—indeed, one biological generation—to another, and take time to change?"

"We don't think it's an *appropriate* consideration," Missouri's representative replied (emphasis added).

SOUTER: "Then I take it you accept it as a fact."

MUNICH: "It may happen."

SOUTER: "If it's a fact, why should it be irrelevant?"

MUNICH: "It's beyond the capacity of the schools to deal with."[8]

That exchange encapsulated one of the root causes of continuing racial divisions in the United States. It dramatized the widespread belief that once laws were passed and court decisions issued to end the legality of racial segregation, the job was done. Nothing else was needed. No responsibility had to be taken for *the effect* of centuries of repression. And African-Americans could and should make their own way in a color-blind society, without further help from anyone, as all other Americans are supposed to have done.

More than two hundred veterans of the civil rights movement met in New London, Connecticut, in late 1994 to recall the great days of the sixties and their epic triumphs in Congress, the courts, and the streets. But those were three decades in the past; in 1994 the old liberals could find little to celebrate.

Herbert Hill, one of the drafters of the Civil Rights Act of 1964, now on the faculty at the University of Wisconsin, made the point Justice Souter had tried to make in his exchange with John Munich, the depressing truth that thirty years had taught. "Abolishing legal racism," Hill said, "does not produce racial equality."

Passage of the Civil Rights Act of 1964 had been a famous victory, said Nicholas de B. Katzenbach, who was attorney general under President Johnson when the 1964 legislation was passed. But in retrospect it was "a drop in a very large bucket" that had done "nothing for the great mass of African-American citizens in this country." Blacks were still subjected to poor education and poor housing and remained victims of high unemployment, Katzenbach said, and were left in a state of such second-rate citizenship that whites continued to "feel they're superior."

Hill agreed that it was "tragic to see what has now happened":

the nation in retreat from racial integration, not least because "the [civil rights] movement failed to eliminate the great disparity in the economic status of blacks and whites."*

In these remarks Hill and Katzenbach pointed to continuing economic deprivation as another principal cause of the tragic failure of racial integration in America. Neither abolition of legal segregation in the South nor political gains elsewhere, for which black and white leaders once held such high hopes, had proved able to end economic disadvantage for blacks or the resulting social discrimination against them.

At about the same time, in Union, South Carolina, a twenty-three-year-old white woman was arrested and charged with murder for drowning her two little boys. She had repeatedly told the nation, even on network television, that the children had been abducted by a black man during a carjacking.

Her description of the abductor had been turned into a police sketch of a man with dark skin that was nationally distributed. Tips from as far away as Seattle, all based on the universal acceptance of the idea that a black man was guilty of a terrible crime, poured into local police and FBI offices.

When Susan Smith's confession of her own guilt disclosed that she had concocted a false charge against a nonexistent black person, Aldon Morris, the African-American head of the social science department at Northwestern University, thought he saw a familiar pattern: "The case demonstrates once again the stereotypical view of black men...that they are...dangerous, that they should be imprisoned. And this...was the same view that guided lynch mobs...that causes black men to be stopped, searched and harassed on a routine basis by the police."

*Hill's and Katzenbach's remarks were reported in *The New York Times*, November 6, 1994, in a brief story relegated to a section called "Region News Briefs." That may have been unintended, but it seems to suggest the relative unimportance today of any serious review of what went wrong with integration.

Many saw in the South Carolina case a parallel to one in Boston in 1989, when a white man told police that his wife had been shot and killed by a black man. Later it developed that the husband was himself the killer, the accused African-American a fiction. The husband committed suicide, but not before dozens of black men had been questioned by police, black housing developments had been "swept" by officers, and one African-American had been arrested and falsely charged with the killing.

Kelvin Pippins, now a hospital orderly, lived as a teenager in 1989 in one of the housing tracts in which Boston police questioned every black man, simply because he was black. Five years later, when Pippins heard of the episode in South Carolina, he thought: "Why'd she have to blame it on a black man? Why not a white male?"

Tyrone Mason, an African-American tennis coach in Chicago, had a ready answer: "She figured if she said a black man did it people would believe her. . . . As long as it's allegedly a black man involved, America will fall for anything."

Louise Taylor, a white school psychologist in South Carolina, conceded that accusing a black "did make [Smith's] story seem more likely." She added: "There's that typical profile of the old bad black guy. We're just too ready to accept that."

Sadly John McCarroll, president of the NAACP chapter in West Spartanburg, South Carolina, near Union, told reporters: "This just points out to us how racism lingers."[9]

Paradoxically, evidences of what seems an improved racial situation abound, and for most talented and able blacks, the situation *is* better than it was in, say, 1960. The abolition of legal segregation in the South is the most prominent example.

The political arena has been opened virtually everywhere. African-Americans have served at the Cabinet level, on the Supreme Court, in the Senate, the House of Representatives, and state legislatures, in municipal offices, as governor of Virginia, and frequently as mayors of major cities. Even Dallas, once a bastion of conservative politics, elected a black mayor in 1995.

The African-American middle class has been substantially expanded, and blacks occupy many high professional positions. Franklin Thomas, for only one example, is president of the Ford Foundation, one of the most prestigious private institutions.

These public evidences of black achievement in a white world are highly misleading. Neither race, in general, regards the other with anything like the amity that might be suggested by, say, the increase (noted in Chapter Eight) in the number of African-American members of Congress. In 1989 Douglas Wilder, a black Democrat, was nineteen points ahead of his white Republican opponent in polls on the day before Virginia's gubernatorial election. Wilder won the next day by about 1 percent. Whites had been reluctant to confess to polltakers that they were not going to vote for an African-American for governor.

Black *and* white candidates in other volatile races have been all too willing to "play the race card," now a political cliché, meaning "to arouse racial attitudes against an opponent of the other color." George Bush's successful presidential campaign of 1988 unabashedly played the race card with the famous Willie Horton commercial. In 1992, with Bush and Bill Clinton appealing to the middle-class vote, the nation's most daunting domestic problem—the poverty- and crime-stricken inner city—went all but unmentioned.

American cities are hotbeds of racial animosities. Racial "incidents" in school buildings and on college campuses are commonplace. Old hate groups have reemerged, and new ones been formed. Worse, evidences of animosity toward or disdain for the other race can be found even among educated middle-class whites and African-Americans.

The emphasis of the press, particularly television, on black violence, even if not deliberately racist and even though black criminality is real, has stimulated anger as well as fear among whites (and not a few blacks). Law-abiding African-Americans often believe that the white-dominated press and television *are* racist, or at least insensitive, and blacks constantly see on TV the "good life" seemingly out of reach for most of their race.

Black economic gains, though real, have gone largely unremarked in the white consciousness, obscured by the fear of the crime-filled inner city that now shapes white stereotypes of African-Americans.

The persisting white notion of white superiority particularly affects affirmative action beneficiaries, who are widely considered to have been given the supposedly un-American advantage of "something for nothing." Their best work is often decried as if it were an accident or an exception that proved some rule of black incapacity. Or such work may be praised *too* highly as if it were remarkable that an African-American should be capable of it.

Blacks moving to better neighborhoods have not found as much change as some might have expected. As pointed out earlier, sales and rental agents have continued to discriminate; combined with white fears of blacks "moving in" and black fears of white resistance, the result is to continue the segregation of the races by housing patterns, in both high-and low-income groups.

Most corporations have opened their lower ranks to African-Americans owing sometimes to affirmative action, sometimes to pressures to appear as "an equal-opportunity employer," less frequently because of black achievement. None of these reasons, however, has caused these companies to admit many African-Americans to their highest offices; in 1995 less than 1 percent of senior executives at Fortune 500 companies were black.

Nothing, moreover, seems to alter the white world's instinctive categorization of male blacks as likely to be violent criminals. Ask Earl G. Graves, Jr., of *Black Enterprise* magazine. Ellis Cose, in his passionate book *The Rage of a Privileged Class*, relates dozens of humiliations of blacks by insensitive or tradition-bound whites.[10]

Ronald Ferguson recalls an instance at Northwestern University when a white man told Fergusen's classmate Glenn Loury that a certain book on mathematics would be over Loury's head. Loury, now an economics professor at Boston University, quickly demonstrated that the book, to him, was relatively elementary. Ferguson recalls that the surprised white was embarrassed—and resented the exposure of his stereotype of a black man who wouldn't understand math.[11]

Vice Chancellor Harold Wallace of the University of North Carolina recalls the case of a black student whose white professor had accused her of plagiarism. The woman took her case to Wallace, also an African-American, but the white professor was convinced of her innocence only when presented with examples of outstanding writing she had done in high school and in other UNC courses.

The white professor admitted to Wallace that he "didn't think black students could write like that."[12]

Perhaps above all, African-Americans continue to suffer from unemployment and economic disadvantage.

Large headlines reported an apparently significant dip in the rate of black unemployment in January 1995. Aided by a slight recovery in manufacturing, the rate fell below 10 percent for the first time in two decades, which was hailed as a triumph.

At 9.8 percent, however, black unemployment was still, as it has been historically, more than twice the white unemployment rate: 4.8 percent. The unemployment rate for black youths aged sixteen to nineteen remained ominously high at 34.6 percent, significantly more than twice the 14.7 rate for whites in that age-group.

The vaunted economic recovery of the nineties, in fact, while important for blacks and whites alike, nevertheless has been badly flawed. Total economic growth from 1991 to 1994 was only about 10 percent, compared with growth that *averaged* nearly 16 percent following each of the recoveries of 1970, 1974, and 1982. Partially as a result, wages adjusted for inflation did not rise in the nineties, as they usually have in past recoveries.

Other factors causing wages to remain at prerecovery levels included cheaper labor abroad and from "temps," the business trend to lay off or not replace workers in order to hold down costs, and the drastic decline of organized labor. If, as some economists believe and all signals indicate, the recovery had passed its peak by early 1995, wage stagnation will continue. And if wages don't rise, the standard of living doesn't either—certainly not for those who were poor or unemployed to begin with.

Anyway, black economic gains in recent years leave much yet to be accomplished. In 1988 about 90 percent of whites had incomes in excess of the poverty level (then sixty-three hundred dollars for a family of four). Only about 60 percent of blacks were at that income level, and of those, fully a third were "near poor"—that is, having incomes less than twice the poverty line.

There has never been a time in American history when as many as half its black citizens have had a household cash income more than twice the poverty level. Nor will such a time soon arrive. As already noted, 43 percent of blacks had incomes at least twice the poverty level in 1987, but that proportion had *dropped* from 47 percent in 1980.[13]

The ingrained white belief in the inferiority of African-Americans noted by Nick Katzenbach at New London may not be racism in the dictionary sense of an ideology of racial superiority, such as motivated the German Nazis against the Jews and others they regarded as "subhuman." Most white Americans would not assert—at least openly—that the black race is genetically inferior; privately or otherwise most would be horrified at the idea of a "final solution" to the American race question (though, unfortunately, some blacks believe and some preach that whites are planning a new Holocaust).

It's commonplace among whites, however, to believe that African-Americans they know or know about, not the entire race, are less industrious, responsible, socially accomplished, educated, and perhaps intelligent than are they and their white friends. Nicholas Lemann sees this pervasive American attitude as "prejudice" rather than "racism," a view that may give faint cause for hope.

In the short run, in daily life, the distinction may make little practical difference. In the long term, however, prejudice may be counteracted, if not overcome, though no one examining race relations in America could be optimistic about that. The phenomenon seems more stubborn than vicious.

The low economic status and undisciplined social behavior of many blacks result in large part from deprived circumstances imposed on them or allowed by whites in the past or the present. But that status and that behavior cause better-off whites to "feel they're superior," in Katzenbach's words. Because they feel superior, they demand that blacks do and be better if they expect to gain equality and respect from the white world.

Most whites are unwilling, however, to suffer inconveniences or to make sacrifices for the advancement of a people they see as inferior and feckless (but threatening), and for whose past history and current situation they feel little responsibility. In self-justification, many come to see such help as, in fact, a hindrance—either destructive of blacks' initiative or wasted on a race incapable of improvement.

So discrimination continues, economic disparity continues, undisciplined behavior continues, social disdain continues, the white sense of superiority continues, and the gulf between the races continues, perhaps even widens.

Neither blacks nor whites can afford to allow this stubborn cycle to keep repeating its course. That way lies continuing second-class status for most blacks and continuing white discrimination against them, continuing fear and insecurity for *both* races, growing national instability, perhaps the violent collision no sensible person wants. Even if the apocalypse does not result, cherished American liberties may well be at risk.

In Chicago in 1994 police, hoping to seize hidden guns, wanted to conduct a sweep search of a housing project terrorized by shooting incidents. Expressing understandable outrage about the shootings and concern for their safety and that of their children, the mostly black residents largely *favored* the sweep. Only the American Civil Liberties Union intervened to stop what would have been a wholesale violation of the constitutional requirement for search warrants.

President Clinton, with his fatal instinct for surrender cloaked in compromise, proposed that those seeking residence in the projects should agree in advance to such searches—in effect, voluntarily surrendering their constitutional rights.

The easy resort to imprisoning African-Americans instead of acting against economic and social ills, moreover, is only a step away from a police roundup. Numerous other protections for citizens against strong-arm law enforcement are under challenge as the fear of crime rises. Even the Supreme Court wants to restrict the right of habeas corpus. Already curfews, which certainly limit citizens' rights and liberty, have been adopted as anticrime measures in several urban jurisdictions. Blacks see such steps as "antiblack," but the real danger is the easy relinquishment, in panic about crime—mostly about *black* crime—of citizens' rights once jealously guarded, perhaps never to be regained if surrendered.

In the mid-sixties—in another world, as it seems now—the nation had seemed on the road to realization of Martin Luther King's dream that someday his children would be judged not by the color of their skins but by "the content of their character," to realization, in fact, of the Republic's claimed but slighted ideals.

Then came backlash, as it was grudgingly realized that having achieved the end of legal segregation in the South, blacks and liberals meant to bring racial integration to the rest of the nation. After 1980 the Reagan-Bush years legitimated the decades during which white America had retreated from the promise embodied in Lyndon Johnson's southern accent when he quoted the black anthem to Congress in 1964: "We shall overcome!"

So, even by 1988, as the Reagan era closed and George Bush prepared to move into the White House, Gary Orfield—a political scientist then at the University of Chicago, now at Harvard—wrote that the flight from integration since Johnson's day had been so precipitate that for all practical purposes *the issue* of economic and social equality for African-Americans had "disappeared from national politics":

The idea that there was something fundamentally wrong that required strong governmental action was rejected. Surveys

193

showed the issue consistently low among white priorities, and reflected a very strong belief among respondents that the problems of discrimination had been solved; indeed, many even felt that *whites* were now the victims of discrimination.[14]

That could be written today, perhaps with more justification. But if racial equality has disappeared as an issue between the mainstream parties, the question of equality remains a divisive, always disturbing element in American life, from which, for neither race, is real escape to be found in angry words or closed eyes.

A disordered period of disappointment, disillusion, fear, anger, and white retreat followed the old racial order of legal segregation and accepted *in*equality. In that period African-Americans, though they made great strides, were not able to close the economic gap with white America, and therefore the white assumption of superiority, the white reluctance to concede that more than legal steps needed to be taken did not change. The growth and behavior of the black underclass then provided a dramatic new cause for white fear and animosity.

After three decades of quick advance and slow retreat, with all but unimaginable numerical diversity swiftly overtaking us, only at mortal peril can the nation continue to tremble along this unjustly drawn black-white fault line. "A house divided against itself cannot stand" in the twentieth any more than in the nineteenth century. And the only route to a more complete American equality is economic advance for most African-Americans, achieved in cooperation with whites rather than at their expense.

In our society, with its dark racial history, its black faces at the bottom of the well, years of partisan political effort may be required to bring about such economic advance and the social leveling that would follow. Today's mainstream parties appear to have neither the will nor the leadership to pursue those goals, even to raise them as issues. Therefore *African-Americans themselves must take the lead, state the goal, and move boldly toward it.*

They cannot achieve it by violence or by separatism or by

greater dependence, either on government or the Democrats. They *may* do it by leading and unifying disparate groups—with interests more common than they realize—into a new political force, dedicated to greater economic and social equality in America.

Unlike the parties that represent us today, such a force would have the potential to achieve real democracy, to change American life by attacking its inequities—perhaps to save us from ourselves.

Notes

Chapter 1: The End of Integration

1. Katharine Q. Seelye, *The New York Times,* January 24, 1995, p. A15.
2. Isabel Wilkerson, *The New York Times,* November 10, 1994.
3. October 20, 1994, p. 1.
4. Derrick Bell, *Faces at the Bottom of the Well: The Permanence of Racism* (New York: Basic Books, 1992). The quotation is from Bell's preface.
5. Nicolaus Mills, *Like a Holy Crusade* (Chicago: Ivan R. Dee, 1992), p. 143.
6. Author's telephone interview with Jesse Jackson, March 1987.

Chapter 2: No Chair in the White House

1. Author's telephone interview with Vernon Jordan, March 1987.
2. Quoted by Randall Kennedy, "Persuasion and Distrust: A Commentary on the Affirmative Action Debate," *Harvard Law Review* (April 1986), p. 1342, fn. 56.
3. David Hamilton, "Poverty Is Still with Us—and Worse," *Quiet Riots*, edited by Fred R. Harris and Roger Wilkins (New York: Pantheon Books, 1988), p. 36.
4. Statistics in this and the following two paragraphs are taken from Kevin Phillips, *The Politics of Rich and Poor* (New York: Random House, 1990), pp. 11, 13, 15, 17.
5. Graph on p. A9, *The New York Times,* August 14, 1995.

6. By the economist Edward N. Wolff of New York University, reported in Keith Bradsher, *The New York Times,* April 17, 1995, p. 1.

7. Ibid., p. D4.

8. Reynolds Farley of the University of Michigan in *Race in America: The Struggle for Equality,* edited by Herbert Hill and James E. Jones, Jr. (Madison: University of Wisconsin Press, 1993), pp. 202–203.

9. Reginald Wilson, "Why the Shortage of Black Professors?," *Journal of Blacks in Higher Education* (Autumn 1993), pp. 25–26.

10. *The State of Black America, 1987,* a report of the Urban League.

11. Author's interview with Eddie N. Williams, March 1987.

12. Margaret C. Simms, *Black Participation in the Post–World War II Economy*, a publication of the Joint Center for Political and Economic Studies, p. 23. Ms. Simms is deputy director of research for the center. Hereafter referred to as *Black Participation.*

13. The section of the *The State of Black America, 1991* entitled "The Economic Status of African-Americans" was written by Dr. David H. Swinton, dean of the School of Business at Jackson State University.

14. Richard L. Berke, *The New York Times,* July 4, 1995, p. 1.

15. As reported on November 12, 1994, by *The New York Times,* in a story by Catherine S. Manegold.

Chapter 3: Mainstream to Nowhere

1. Jesse Jackson, *New Perspectives Quarterly* (Summer 1991), pp. 12, 15. Hereafter referred to as *NPQ* Summer '91.

2. *The Washington Post,* November 12, 1994, p. A3, quoted in a story by William Claiborne.

3. David C. Ruffin, *Focus*, the monthly magazine of the Joint Center for Political and Economic Studies (May 1992), p. 3.

4. So he referred in retirement to the war in Vietnam. Doris Kearns, *Lyndon Johnson and the American Dream* (New York: New American Library, 1977).

5. Michael Frisby, *The Wall Street Journal,* February 6, 1995, p. A1. Frisby identified the respondent as Linda Faye Williams, director of the Black Caucus Foundation's research institute. She later told the *Journal*: "People like to talk about the angry white male but what doesn't get discussed is how angry blacks are too."

Chapter 4: Liberal vs. Conservative

1. Isabel Wilkerson, *The New York Times,* November 10, 1994.
2. *The Washington Post,* May 11, 1995, op-ed page.
3. Wilkerson, op. cit.
4. Ibid. The remark Wilkins remembered was made before Colin Powell emerged as a possible presidential candidate, then decided not to run.
5. Gerald F. Seib, *The Wall Street Journal,* May 11, 1994, p. A16. The Dawson-Brown survey was not an ordinary poll but consisted of forty-five-minute interviews with each of 1,206 respondents.
6. Wilkins's conversation with the author, May 11, 1994.

Chapter 5: Expanding the Center

1. Quoted by Eddie N. Williams and Milton D. Morris, "Racism and Our Future," *Race in America,* p. 422. Attributed to Kenneth Clark and John Hope Franklin, *The Nineteen Eighties: Prologue and Prospect* (Washington, D.C.: Joint Center for Political Studies, 1981), p. 19.
2. David W. Dunlap, *The New York Times*, December 4, 1994, p. 8, continued from p. 1 of the real estate section.
3. David Aldridge, *The Washington Post,* December 16, 1995, pp. A1, A18.
4. A contribution to *Race in America,* p. 18.
5. According to a study by Gary Solon, an economist at the University of Michigan.
6. Author's interview with H. L. Gates, the director of the Harvard black studies program, May 13, 1993.
7. *The Wall Street Journal,* May 4, 1995, p. A6.
8. Matt Murray, *The Wall Street Journal,* May 4, 1995, p. A1.
9. Edmund L. Andrews, *The New York Times,* January 3, 1996, p. 1.
10. Murray, op. cit.
11. Nicholas Lemann, *The Promised Land* (New York: Vintage Books, 1992).
12. "Chasing the Dream," *NPQ* Summer '91, p. 33.
13. The Harvard panel discussion took place on May 6, 1993.
14. Lemann, *NPQ* Summer '91, p. 35.

Chapter 6: How Level the Field?

1. Author's interview with John Hope Franklin, December 4, 1993.
2. Stampp quoted the editor in his acceptance speech in New York for the Lincoln Prize, awarded for his life's work, February 11, 1993.

3. Author's interview with Randall Kennedy, May 18, 1993.

4. Author's interview with David Evans, April 5, 1993.

5. Kenneth Clark, *Dark Ghetto: Dilemmas of Social Power* (New York: Harper and Row, 1965), p. 22.

6. Hamilton, op. cit., p. 36.

7. Susan Mayer and Christopher Jencks, "War on Poverty: No Apologies, Please," *The New York Times,* November 9, 1995, op-ed page.

8. Andrew Hacker, *Two Nations: Black and White, Separate, Hostile, Unequal* (New York: Ballantine Books, 1992), p. 214.

9. Speech in Washington to the 140th Indiana Regiment, March 17, 1865.

10. Author's interview with Dr. Alvin Poussaint, a psychiatrist at the Baker Children's Center of Children's Hospital in Boston, March 2, 1993.

11. Kenneth Clark, "Racial Progress and Retreat: A Personal Memoir," *Race in America*, p. 17.

12. Quoted in *Journal of Blacks in Higher Education* (Winter 1993–94), p. 70.

13. Author's interview with H. L. Gates, May 13, 1993.

14. *Black Participation*, Figure 1, p. 3.

15. *Journal of Blacks in Higher Education* (Autumn 1993), pp. 25–26.

Chapter 7: Feeding the Backlash

1. Author's interview with Alvin Poussaint, March 2, 1993.

2. For the percentages of black and white pupils in various cities' public schools, all 1984 figures, *Quiet Riots,* Tables 6.3 and 6.5. For the new anti-integration campaign, Peter Applebome, *The New York Times*, September 26, 1995, p. 1 continued to p. A21.

3. The commission is a bipartisan panel of ten Democrats and ten Republicans, chaired by Secretary of Labor Robert Reich. It conducted numerous hearings and private interviews with business leaders and also relied extensively on 1990 Census Bureau data. Peter T. Kilbourn, *The New York Times,* March 16, 1995, p. A22.

4. Quoted in an introduction, by Margaret C. Simms, editor, to *Economic Perspectives on Affirmative Action* (Washington, D.C.: Joint Center for Political and Economic Studies), p. 3.

5. Cited in a memorandum to "members of Congress" from Ralph G. Neas of the Leadership Conference on Civil Rights, Washington, D.C., March 30, 1995.

6. William L. Taylor, *Poverty & Race* (Washington, D.C.: Poverty and Race Research Action Council, May–June 1995), pp. 2, 3

Notes

7. U.S. Equal Employment Opportunity Division figures, reprinted in *Blacks and Whites: Can We All Get Along?*, a bound reproduction of articles from the *Indianapolis Star,* February 21–28, 1993, p. 13.
8. Todd S. Purdum, *The New York Times,* March 10, 1995, p. 1.
9. Ibid.
10. Statement prepared for the Congressional Black Caucus, March 16, 1995. Representative Waters is co-chair of the caucus task force on affirmative action.
11. Steven A. Holmes, *The New York Times,* March 16, 1995, p. 1.
12. March 1, 1995. Steele is the author of *The Content of Our Character* (New York: St. Martin's Press, 1990).

Chapter 8: Majority and Minority

1. Both remarks were made at a Supreme Court hearing on "majority-minority" congressional districts in Georgia and Louisiana. Steven A. Holmes, *The New York Times,* April 20, 1995, p. A20.
2. David Bositis, *Redistricting and Representation* (Washington, D.C.: Joint Center for Political and Economic Studies, 1995), p. 25 (proof copy).
3. Both remarks were quoted in Steven A. Holmes, *The New York Times,* June 30, 1995, p. A23.

Chapter 9: "A Term Devoid of Hope"

1. Ms. Harris spoke at a conference on criminal justice at Dana College in Nebraska on April 17, 1993.
2. William Julius Wilson, Robert Aponte, Joleen Kirschenman, and Loic J. D. Wacquant, "The Ghetto Underclass and the Changing Structure of Urban Poverty," *Quiet Riots,* p. 112. This chapter is hereafter referred to as Wilson et al.
3. Hamilton, op. cit., pp. 16–17.
4. Ronald B. Mincy and Susan J. Wiener, *The Under Class in the 1980s: Changing Concept, Constant Reality* (Washington, D.C.: Urban Institute, 1993). Hereafter cited as *Under Class.*
5. Wilson et al., p. 112.
6. *Under Class,* p. 8.
7. Wilson, *NPQ* Summer '91, p. 26.
8. Charles Murray, *Losing Ground: American Social Policy, 1950–1980* (New York: Basic Books, 1984).
9. From Jean Harris's Dana College speech.

10. Douglas Massey, *NPQ* Summer '91, p. 33.
11. Gary Orfield, *Quiet Riots*, pp. 105–106.
12. Glazer made these remarks on March 24, 1993.
13. Wilson et al., p. 135.
14. *Under Class*, pp. 6–7.

Chapter 10: Throwing Away the Key

1. This and all previous and following quotations from President Clinton's Memphis speech are taken from excerpts transcribed by the Federal Information Systems Corporation and published by *The New York Times* on November 14, 1993.
2. Sermon, April 4, 1967, Riverside Cathedral, New York City. Dr. King made much the same statement to the annual meeting of the Southern Christian Leadership Conference in Louisville, Kentucky, a week later.
3. *Under Class*, Table 3.
4. Brent Staples, "Into the White Ivory Tower," *The New York Times Magazine*, February 6, 1994, p. 36. The article was a prepublication excerpt from *Parallel Time: Growing Up in Black and White* (New York: Pantheon Books, 1994).
5. Author's interview with John Hope Franklin, December 4, 1993.
6. David Stout, *The New York Times*, May 9, 1995, p. B1. Graves is the son of Earl G. Graves, Sr., the nationally known chief executive of *Black Enterprise*. Coincidentally, the senior Graves is leading a group of prominent African-Americans in defending affirmative action programs.
7. Jann Wenner and William Greider, *Rolling Stone* (December 9, 1993), p. 45.
8. David Johnston, *The New York Times,* February 16, 1994, p. 1.
9. The preceding three paragraphs are based on a speech at the Dana College conference on criminal justice, April 17, 1993, by the noted criminologist Norval Morris, a former dean of the University of Chicago Law School.
10. Department of Justice figures, reported by *The New York Times,* October 28, 1994, p. 1. The Sentencing Project, a Washington prison survey group, counts prison and jail inmates together and puts the resulting U.S. "rate of incarceration" at 519 per 100,000 of population.
11. From Morris's Dana College speech.
12. Katherine Tate, *From Protest to Politics: The New Black Voters in*

American Elections (Cambridge, Mass.: Harvard University Press and the Russell Sage Foundation, 1993).

13. Author's interview with Katherine Tate, May 11, 1993.

14. Jeffrey Abramson, an authority on juries, pointed out these disparities in "Making the Law Color Blind," an op-ed article in *The New York Times,* October 16, 1995, p. A15.

15. Seth Mydans, *The New York Times*, December 8, 1993, p. 1.

16. Fox Butterfield, *The New York Times*, August 13, 1995, p. 1.

17. Department of Justice figures as of June 30, 1994. Inmates in local jails are not included.

18. These facts about imprisonment were provided by the Sentencing Project and were published on the op-ed page of *The New York Times,* January 9, 1991, in an article by the author.

19. Norval Morris at Dana College.

20. The Justice Department study was reported by Bob Herbert in *The New York Times,* December 19, 1993, p. 13. The surge in handgun sales after the Long Island Rail Road shooting was reported on p. 1 of the same issue, in a story by B. D. Ayres, Jr.

21. Tammy Audeh, *The New York Times,* June 21, 1995.

22. John Whitley's speech was reported by Colman McCarthy, *The Washington Post,* December 3, 1994, p. A17.

Chapter 11: Middle-Class Blues

1. Author's telephone interview with Vernon Jordan, December 19, 1992.

2. Wilson, *NPQ* Summer '91.

3. Reynolds Farley, *Race in America,* pp. 200–203, Fig. 9 (U.S. Census Bureau).

4. Orfield, *Quiet Riots,* p. 96.

5. Wilson, *NPQ* Summer '91.

6. Charles Hamilton was interviewed by the author by telephone on December 21, 1993. Shirley Chisholm was interviewed by Mike Wallace on *60 Minutes,* Columbia Broadcasting System, June 7, 1981.

7. William Julius Wilson, *The Truly Disadvantaged: The Inner City, the Underclass and Public Policy* (Chicago: University of Chicago Press, 1987), p. 61.

8. Ira Berkow, *The New York Times,* April 20, 1993. Jalen Rose now plays for the Denver Nuggets of the NBA.

9. Author's interview with Randall Kennedy, May 18, 1993.

10. Author's interview with Ronald Ferguson, April 26, 1993. Ferguson

found Hispanic students falling behind in the first grade, then staying behind.

11. Wallace Kaufman, "Racism and the BCC Controversy," *Carolina Alumni Review* (Winter 1992), p. 29.

12. Eight hundred black journalists were randomly selected from NABJ membership lists and surveyed by mail; 537 responses were tabulated by *USA Today*. A random sample also was taken from membership rolls of the American Society of Newspaper Editors, the Radio and Television News Directors Association, and the American Society of Magazine Editors. One hundred of those selected responded to the survey.

Chapter 12: Speeches and Spokesmen

1. The Deer Park incident and its aftermath were reported in *The New York Times* on November 13 and 16, 1993. The Mundy affair was covered in *The Washington Post* on November 12 and 16, 1993, nearly two weeks after Mundy appeared on *60 Minutes* on October 31.

2. *NPQ* Summer '91, p. 30.

3. Erna Smith, a faculty member at San Francisco State College, while a fellow at the Joan Shorenstein Barone Center at Harvard, conducted a detailed study of television coverage of the Los Angeles riots of 1992. She cited the "Latinization" of American cities as a major development.

4. Ibid.

5. Ibid.

6. These remarks were made at a seminar on March 24, 1993.

Chapter 13: Tragic Failure

1. *NPQ* Summer '91, p. 15.

2. Ibid., p. 29.

3. The author interviewed Dr. Counter and saw the model of the monument on April 8, 1993.

4. From a printed transcript of the proceedings of the Thirteenth Annual *Providence Journal*/Brown University Public Affairs Conference, March 2–11, 1993, p. 34.

5. In a review of Thomas Sowell, *Ethnic America: A History*. Huggins's review appeared in the *Yale Review* (Autumn 1982), p. 84.

6. July 1, 1993.

7. *NPQ* Summer '91, p. 32.

8. Linda Greenhouse, *The New York Times*, January 12, 1995, p. A18.

9. These responses to the South Carolina case, including that of Alvin Poussaint, were reported in *The New York Times*, November 4, 1994, p. 1, in a story by Rick Bragg; and in the *Times* of November 6, 1994, in a story by Don Terry.

10. Ellis Cose, *The Rage of a Privileged Class* (New York: HarperCollins, 1993).

11. Author's interview with Ronald Ferguson, April 20, 1993.

12. Wallace Kaufman, "Racism and the BCC Controversy," *Carolina Alumni Review* (Winter 1992), p. 21.

13. The last two paragraphs are from Farley, *Race in America*, pp. 201–203.

14. Orfield, *Quiet Riots*, p. 91.

Index

Index

Bennett, William, 43
Berke, Richard, 2
Bilbo, Theodore, 16n
Birmingham, Ala., 80, 103, 108
birthrate, 129n
Bitburg Cemetery, 11
Black Caucus, 16, 46, 111, 118, 172, 173
Black Enterprise, 139
black families, disintegration of, 4, 5, 123–124
Black Leadership Forum, 16–17
Black Panthers, 8, 90–91
Black Power (Hamilton), 157
black power movement, 8, 89–92
blacks:
   in athletics, 5, 8, 88, 159, 161
   on college faculties, 20, 74–75
   Democratic party and, xii-xiii, 3, 7, 30, 34, 35–36, 37–42, 46–50, 97, 121
   economic status of, x, 34, 41–42, 58, 59, 131–132, 190–192; *see also* family income
   effects of Republican economic policies on, 17–24, 58
   ethnic communities of, 4
   failure of political gains to lead to economic improvement for, xii, 3–4, 57–59, 187–188
   generational differences among, 50, 89–90
   in House of Representatives, 106, 107, 110–111; *see also* Black Caucus
   immigrant experience compared with, 181–184
   importance of economic power for, 58–60, 62–64, 194
   Jews and, 97, 168–174
   military performance of, 168, 172
   moral responsibility urged upon by Clinton, 24–25, 40, 135–136
   population of, 4, 111, 142
   postwar northern migration of, 70, 130, 175–176
   prison population of, x, 4, 141–142
   proposed removal from North America of, 76
   Republican party support from, 36–37, 47–48

sensationalist media image of, 4, 58–59, 137–138, 178, 188
Simpson's acquittal, reactions to, ix, x, 146–147
third political party seen as hope for, xiii, 29, 34, 41–42, 60, 195
use of term, xn, 89
see also African-Americans; middle class, black; race; underclass
black separatism, 8
black voting-age population (BVAP), 110–111, 113, 116, 117–118
black-white relations:
   black power movement and, 90–92
   black resentment of whites in, 97
   "level playing field" myth and, 83
   underclass and, 129–130
   as underlying election issue, 1–3, 21, 46, 97, 99–100, 188
   on university campuses, 162–163
   white attitudes in, 74, 77–78, 79, 84–86, 188–190, 191
   white fear of blacks in, 1, 4, 9, 10, 13, 21, 35, 97–98, 137–141
   white recognition of "American-ness" of blacks and, 183–184
   widening gap in, ix-xiii, 35, 166, 192
   see also integration; racism; slavery
black youth culture, 160–161
Blair House, 17
blue-collar workers, 61–62, 124–125
B'nai B'rith, 171
Bob Jones University, 15
Boggs, Lindy, 112
Bolick, Clint, 104
Bositis, David A., 109n
Boston, Mass., 10, 87, 95, 124, 147, 179, 187
Boston Globe, The, 151
Boyz N the Hood, 154
Bradley, Bill, 44, 45, 48–49, 54–55
Brooklyn Dodgers, 88
Brotherhood of Sleeping Car Porters, 37n
Brown, H. Rap, 8, 90
Brown, Ron, 41
Brown, Ronald, 50
Brown v. *Board of Education of Topeka, Kansas,* 20, 78, 92, 95
budget, federal, balancing of, 25, 27, 41, 68–69

Index

Index

Index